THE NEW BABY

ANSWERBOOK™

From Birth to Kindergarten, Answers to the Top 150 Questions about Raising a Young Child

10/09

THE NEW BABY

ANSWERBOOK™

From Birth to Kindergarten, Answers to the Top 150 Questions about Raising a Young Child

ROBIN GOLDSTEIN, PhD, WITH JANET GALLANT

SOURCEBOOKS, INC.®
NAPERVILLE, ILLINOIS

Published by Sourcebooks, Inc.
P.O. Box 4410, Naperville, Illinois 60567–4410
(630) 961–3900
Fax: (630) 961–2168
www.sourcebooks.com

Library of Congress Cataloging-in-Publication Data
Goldstein, Robin.
The new baby answer book : from birth to kindergarten, answers to the top 150 questions about raising a young child / Robin Goldstein with Janet Gallant.
p. cm.
1. Toddlers. 2. Preschool children. 3. Child rearing. I. Gallant, Janet. II. Title.

HQ774.5.G66 2009
649.'123—dc22

2008034037

Printed and bound in the United States of America.
CHG 10 9 8 7 6 5 4 3 2 1

Dedication

*With great appreciation and so much love—to my husband Miles,
my children Ari and Anna, and my parents Cynthia and Rez.*

Contents

Acknowledgments

This mission—answering parents' questions and helping them gain a better understanding of their children—could not have been realized without the help and encouragement of family, friends, and colleagues. Thanks so much to Nina Graybill for her guidance in directing me to Sourcebooks; Sara Appino and Deb Werksman for all their assistance and for taking this project on; Andy Gallant for his support and technical know-how; Janet Gallant for her unfailing help, her way with words, and her friendship, which I so greatly value; my husband Miles for all his love, support, and encouragement; and my children Ari and Anna, who continue to teach me the deepest meaning of love.

Introduction

"Should I pick my baby up when he cries?"

"Do I always have to be consistent?"

"Why won't my child cooperate in the morning?"

"How can I teach my child to be more responsible?"

"What about shyness?"

"What can I do about picky eating?"

"Is it okay to bribe children?"

Raising children is a vitally important job that can be difficult, demanding, and exciting all at the same time. Your questions will range from the mundane (cleanup, holding still during a diaper change, and dropping food from the high chair) to the complex (teaching right from wrong, sibling rivalry, weaning, choosing the best nursery school or day care, kindergarten readiness, learning to feel self-confident, and dealing with divorce).

The New Baby Answer Book answers the questions parents have asked me most frequently in my many years in practice advising parents and educators on childhood development. You'll find workable solutions to problems as well as insights into children's thinking, based on the work of renowned child development researcher Jean Piaget.

You'll also find a great deal of reassurance. As you learn about typical experiences and the predictable stages of development (as defined by psychosocial theorist Erik Erikson), you'll find that most of your child's behavior is perfectly normal. Young children are strong-willed, have bedtime struggles, need reminders, have fears, use bathroom language, and have trouble sharing. You'll be able to form realistic expectations and eliminate many of the conflicts that come from anticipating, for example, that your two- or three-year-old will act as a four- or five-year-old would.

This book encourages you to spend time with your child, listening to him, setting limits, and taking an interest. Your child will benefit in every way and at every stage from your love and active involvement. Even if some or most of his care is provided by others, parenting, of course, is truly your responsibility. Therefore, the answers are addressed to you, the parent, although the advice also applies to all the caregivers, teachers, and other adults involved in your child's life.

The questions and answers often alternate the use of each gender. However, the answers for the most part apply to either gender. Similarly, the answers generally speak of parents dealing with one child, but the advice is applicable to families with any number of children.

Getting specific answers to your child-rearing questions is important because you want to do the best you can for your child. Your day-to-day actions and attitudes can guide your child's character and behavior in positive ways. The challenging job of parenting requires love, sacrifice, time, and attention, and you deserve all the help and encouragement you can get. *The New Baby Answer Book* acknowledges your natural frustrations and uncertainty and gives you reassurance and answers to make parenting easier, more successful, and more enjoyable.

Chapter 1

THE FIRST YEAR

- When will my baby sleep through the night?
- Which toys are best for babies?
- Is it normal to feel guilty or upset by a crying baby?
- What should I look for in a good pediatrician?
- What questions should I ask a potential pediatrician?
- Should I schedule my baby's feedings or feed on demand?
- Is my child too dependent on me?
- Should I pick my baby up when she cries?
- What should I do if my baby needs constant comforting?
- Is my baby "good"?
- How long will my baby be anxious around strangers?
- Is it okay if my baby is attached to a blanket or other objects?
- Should I give my child a pacifier?
- Why won't my child hold still during diaper changes?
- How much childproofing should I do?
- How can I keep my child safe when he wants to explore?
- What should I do when my child touches things at other people's houses?
- When will my child's desire to touch everything end?
- My child puts everything in her mouth. What can I do?
- When should I wean?
- Out of sight, out of mind—does every baby think this way?
- When will my baby begin to crawl?
- How can I keep my crawling baby safe?
- When will my child start walking?
- Is it frustrating to go places with a child who's learning to walk?

When will my baby sleep through the night?

"Does your baby sleep through the night?" That's a question you probably dread answering if your baby is still waking up. Many people believe that a baby should be sleeping through the night by the time he's three months old, so if your baby isn't, you may naturally feel frustrated and worried. Losing sleep is one of the hardest adjustments new parents have to make.

Actually, it's rare for an infant to consistently sleep through the night. Some babies do, but many are still waking up at ten months and others are two or three years old before they sleep all night. The frequency of waking varies from child to child and depends on many circumstances.

An infant may wake up at night to be fed, changed, or held. A slightly older baby may turn himself over during the night, waking up in the process. If a baby has new teeth coming in, he may be uncomfortable and wake up to be comforted. And if he's developmentally at the stage when he believes people exist only if he can see them, he may wake up to see his parents and be reassured. Parents sometimes consider this last type of wakefulness to be manipulative because their baby stops crying as soon as they come into his room. But he doesn't intend to manipulate—he just wants to see his parents and be close to them.

Basically, your baby wakes up because he needs to be comforted, fed, or helped. He doesn't understand that you prefer to meet his needs during the day and sleep during the night.

A wakeful baby can be difficult and frustrating. If you get up at night to respond to your baby, you lose sleep and suffer the physical and emotional consequences of being tired. You may also face the criticism of others: "The only way your baby is going to learn to sleep is if you let him cry it out." Such comments are unfortunate, because parents who do get up at night with their child need support and encouragement. Many parents eventually become secretive about getting up because they don't want to be ridiculed by friends and relatives.

Which toys are best for babies?

An infant likes to look at objects around him. By three to four months, he may be accidentally batting toys with his hands or feet, and by four to six months he may intentionally try to touch and grasp objects. During the earliest months you can hang mobiles from your baby's crib or ceiling, put a safe mirror against the side of the crib, or secure a colorful pinwheel to the hood of the baby stroller. Once he can grasp objects, you can provide soft, non-toxic toys that can safely go in his mouth and that won't harm him if he bumps against them: a rattle or squeaking toy, teething beads, or toys with faces.

Once your baby can sit up, attach a busy box to the side of his crib. He'll enjoy one with buttons, dials, pop-ups, and other things he can control. You can also give him kitchen items to play with such as plastic bowls and spoons, and a spill-proof container with a little water that he can shake and watch. When he can crawl, put these kitchen items in a low cupboard so he can easily get to them. He'll also like musical toys, stuffed animals, squeeze toys, soft cars and trucks, large balls, and cloth or cardboard books. You can make books for him by slipping pictures of your family and things he likes into a photo album.

Is it normal to feel guilty or upset by a crying baby?

Sometimes parents of a wakeful baby become resentful, envying other parents whose child sleeps through the night and wondering what's wrong with their own child. "Does everyone else have easier babies?" Parents may blame themselves for their situation, believing that they caused their baby's wakefulness by being too attentive to his cries. "If only we had let him cry it out earlier, maybe we'd all be sleeping now." There's really no need for doubt and self-blame. When you go to your baby at night, you give him a sense of security and a sense that his needs will consistently be met. When a baby is left to cry it out at night, he gives up and cries himself back to sleep. It's really okay to go to your baby when he wakes up crying. Parents of a wakeful baby need to know that they're not alone. Many babies wake up during the night. Once parents understand this—that they're not alone—they can alter their expectations about normal sleeping patterns and begin to feel better about their child's behavior.

If you're the parent of a wakeful baby, you'll want to help him get back to sleep as quickly as possible. First, try to meet his needs by changing him, feeding him, or making him more comfortable. If he's still wakeful, try soothing him with rocking or singing. Sometimes mechanical, repetitive sounds are calming—the sound of the ocean; running water; the hum of a hair dryer, fan, or vacuum cleaner. There are special sound machines, CDs, and toys that play the sounds of heartbeats; you might try one of these. Having him sleep with you may be less exhausting and frustrating than getting up several times to comfort and feed him.

If you're not getting enough sleep, try napping during the day or early evening, or going to bed early at night. And recognize that, as exhausting as this can be, wakefulness will decrease as your child gets older.

What should I look for in a good pediatrician?

Every parent wants a pediatrician who's dependable, competent, caring, and easy to talk to. Some doctors are all of these things, and others are not. Therefore, when you're looking for a pediatrician, you should (to the extent allowed by your insurance) take the time to visit a couple of doctors, seek recommendations, and ask questions.

To get the names of pediatricians you can interview, ask for recommendations from friends, relatives, your obstetrician, doula or midwife, and your insurance company. Once you have the names of a few pediatricians, set up appointments to visit. It's always best to see at least two doctors so you can compare them before you make your decision. Some charge for consultations, so ask about fees.

When you visit each pediatrician's office, look around. Are there toys and books available for children? Is the floor clean enough for a baby to crawl on? Are sick and healthy children separated? Are the receptionists, physician assistants, and nurses pleasant?

When you talk to the doctor, ask questions, and pay attention to how she responds. Does she answer you fully, in terms you can understand, and does she listen to your point of view? Do you feel comfortable with her? How do you think she relates to children?

Because your relationship with a pediatrician will be a long and involved one, it's important to choose a doctor carefully.

What questions should I ask a potential pediatrician?

Here are some questions you might want to ask during an interview with a potential pediatrician: Where and when will the pediatrician examine your newborn? How does she feel about breast feeding and bottle feeding, and does she approve of the feeding method you've chosen? Does she make herself available to discuss non-medical issues such as pacifier use, sleeping habits, and nutrition? Does she have regular call-in hours when you can ask questions over the phone? Does the practice offer advice and medical updates through a website? Is there a fee for phone consultations?

As you consider which pediatrician to use, think about such practical issues as the distance from the office to your home, the office hours (some pediatricians have extended hours for working parents), the doctor's fees, her procedure for emergency visits, and how her office handles insurance. If she practices alone, find out who covers for her when she's sick or on vacation, and try to meet that doctor briefly. If the pediatrician you interview is part of a group practice, ask if you can choose one of the doctors as your primary pediatrician.

Choose a doctor you feel comfortable talking to, since you'll frequently consult with her about your child's growth and development, as well as medical problems. You may find that after you start taking your child to a pediatrician, your feelings about that doctor will change. You may not have known at the time you first interviewed her that you would be facing such issues as thumb-sucking, sleep problems, or late toilet use.

You may discover that her opinions about these issues are contrary to yours. She may, for example, be against giving bottles to a toddler, while you think it's acceptable.

In such situations, parents who feel intimidated by their pediatrician choose to hide their child's habits when they come in for appointments. They may leave their child's blanket, pacifier, or bottle at home, rather than face the doctor's disapproval. Such parents may eventually grow distant from their pediatrician, seeking her advice only on medical issues. Other parents in the same situation may become more open with their doctor, letting her know just how their child behaves and discussing differences of opinion on parenting issues. If you find yourself disagreeing with your child's doctor too often, you'll have to decide whether to work out a compromise or switch pediatricians and start a new relationship.

Should I schedule my baby's feedings or feed on demand?

Infants don't have the ability to control or postpone their needs. If they're hungry or need to be comforted, they desire immediate gratification. When you respond to your infant's cries, providing food and comfort, your baby begins to trust her world and to feel some small ability to affect what happens to her. If her cries for food are ignored, she has no way to satisfy herself.

Feeding your infant on demand, which means whenever your baby begins to fuss, is one way you can meet your baby's needs. Demand-fed babies and their parents are usually calmer and more content than families with babies who are fed on a schedule. This is because an infant fed on demand does less crying for food and comfort, and her parents spend less time distracting her since she doesn't have to be held off until a scheduled feeding. A demand-fed baby also may be easier to put to sleep since she can be soothed with nursing or a bottle when she seems tired. There's no chance of overfeeding a demand-fed baby; an infant will not drink more than she wants or needs.

Parents who don't choose to feed their baby on demand, but rather on a schedule, may find themselves unsuccessfully trying to comfort or distract their crying baby. Your baby might want to be fed, but you may think that she should wait three or four hours because she's "just been fed." Since it's often hard for parents to listen to their baby cry, this can be a difficult situation, and one that probably takes as much time and energy as the extra feedings given to a demand-fed baby. While it's true that some babies can wait four hours between feedings, it's equally true that some babies need feeding much more frequently.

New parents often decide to feed their baby on a schedule because of advice from friends, relatives, and their pediatrician. In the face of such advice, parents may find it difficult to trust their instincts and begin demand feeding. They also worry that demand feeding means giving in to their child and letting her have too much control. Yet an infant, because she's helpless, needs to feel she has some control and some ability to make other people respond.

The decision to demand-feed or feed on a schedule is often influenced by the way a baby is fed—by breast or bottle. Although either method can be adapted to scheduled or demand feeding, it's more likely that a breast-fed baby will be demand-fed, if only because of the ease of feeding. A mother can easily offer her breast at any time, while the parents of a bottle-fed infant must first prepare and warm bottles.

A bottle-fed infant is more likely to be fed on a schedule, because her parents can easily see how much milk she's drinking and thus can decide when they think she's had enough. Parents of a breast-fed baby, on the other hand, don't know how much their baby is drinking. When she cries soon after nursing, her mother is likely to offer the breast again because she may not have had enough milk at the last feeding.

You can be successful breast feeding or bottle feeding, but using either method, you'll satisfy your baby best if you feed her on demand. If you feel you must follow a schedule, be flexible. When comforting doesn't work between scheduled feedings, your baby's cries probably mean she's hungry or so tired she needs to soothe herself to sleep with a feeding. At such times, ignore the clock, follow your instincts, and meet your baby's needs.

Is my child too dependent on me?

Many new parents are surprised at how much time, attention, and effort raising a child involves. When they discover that their baby is naturally demanding and dependent, they sometimes worry about "giving in" to his needs. If they pick him up when he cries, offer a bottle or breast on demand, or keep him near throughout the day, will he soon become too dependent? In our society, independence is viewed as a positive trait, and many parents are concerned if their babies seem too attached to people. Yet, when parents fully understand their child's dependency needs, they can see there's no need to worry about their baby's lack of self-sufficiency.

Infants and young children are almost totally dependent on adults; this is a natural and necessary condition of early childhood. It's normal for your baby to want the constant comfort of being held, fed, changed, loved, and played with, and there's nothing harmful about giving in these ways to your young child. A child whose needs are met and who has a strong attachment to his parents develops a foundation of trust and security that will allow him to gradually become independent.

Some parents feel that it's never too soon to start teaching their child to become independent: "He's going to have to learn sometime that he can't always have his way." "He has to find out what life is really like." And some parents believe that giving in to a child's needs in infancy will make it that much harder to get him to give up his dependencies later on.

Parents who are uneasy about how dependent their young child is may, in an attempt to foster independence, make conscious decisions not to meet all of his needs. They may hesitate to pick him up when he cries, or hold back on cuddling or frequent nursing. They may feel guilty and full of self-doubt whenever they do give more than they think they should.

However, if your baby learns to trust your care and support, he'll turn into a toddler who explores his surroundings with confidence. And as he grows, his natural drive for independence will begin to show. A ten-month-old will want to feed himself, a two-year-old will cry out, "I'll do it myself," a three-year-old will feel good going off on his tricycle, and a five-year-old will happily spend time with his friends.

Your young child will always have a strong need to be cared for, of course, but as he gets older, he'll become more and more independent. Although there will be times when your child temporarily becomes more dependent—when he enters preschool, if your family moves, when a sibling is born—if his early dependency needs have been met, he'll move into the world with a greater sense of trust and confidence.

Should I pick my baby up when she cries?

Crying is a baby's way of communicating. Particularly in the early months, a baby cries when she's hungry, cold, wet, tired, or wants to be held and played with. Between six and nine months, she may cry—particularly at night—because she doesn't understand that her parents exist unless she sees them. Babies know the world as either pleasurable or uncomfortable; when their needs are met, they feel good, and when they aren't, they feel badly and cry.

You may wonder how you should respond when your baby cries. If you pick her up each time, will her demands increase? Is there a chance she'll become spoiled? Parents who wish to follow their instincts and respond to their baby's tears often are confused by people who say, "Don't pick her up; you'll spoil her," "Let her cry; it's good for her lungs," or "You can't always be there for her."

The truth is that picking up your crying baby won't spoil her. Rather, it will help her develop a sense of security that will actually make her less likely to cry in the long run. Babies whose cries bring a helpful response begin to anticipate that whenever they cry, someone will respond. This cause-and-effect connection gives a baby a secure and comfortable feeling and also teaches her to trust her parents. Learning to trust is a critical part of early development. If parents respond erratically and unpredictably to their baby's cries, their baby will sense that there's little she can do to affect her environment. In such a situation, she'll learn to feel insecure and mistrust those around her.

Of course, there's a wide range of parental behavior between the extremes of total responsiveness and unresponsiveness. No matter how hard you try to calm and comfort your baby, there will be times when she'll remain frustrated. But if you're consistently caring during the early months, your baby will start life with a sense of trust.

What should I do if my baby needs constant comforting?

Comforting a crying baby is very important, but it can also be difficult, especially if a baby cries often or during a busy moment. If you find that your baby needs a lot of comforting during the day, use a cloth infant carrier that will let you hold your baby close while leaving your hands free. The contact and constant movement can be very soothing.

If your baby does a lot of crying at night, you may feel frustrated and unsure how to respond. Your natural instinct may be to pick her up and feed her, but you also may be tired, and you may be getting negative advice. Your pediatrician might advise you to let your child "cry it out." Many people advocate ignoring a baby's cries in the hope that she'll learn to sleep through the night. One theory says that if parents refuse to comfort or feed their baby during the night, she'll stop crying after twenty minutes to an hour and go back to sleep. After many days or weeks of this routine, she'll no longer wake up at night.

Although the prospect of an evening of uninterrupted sleep may certainly be attractive to you, when you comfort your baby, you let her know that she can depend on you. When you hold and soothe her, you give her a sense of certainty that you'll be there when she needs you.

Is my baby "good"?

Is a "good" baby one who sleeps a lot and doesn't cry much? Most people say "yes," and their answer is understandable. "Good" and "fussy" are judgmental terms people often use to describe the behavior and temperament of a baby.

Parents often believe that their child is a reflection of them. They want a content baby who's easy to care for and who gives them a feeling of success. And many parents feel bad if their baby cries or has colic. Labeling and judging babies for their behavior isn't useful because they're only expressing their needs in the best way they can. When babies cry and fuss, they're telling their parents that something's wrong. They're tired, hurt, uncomfortable, hungry, wet, scared, or needing to be held.

Labeling babies begins very early. One new mother was told by a maternity nurse that her hungry infant had been crying in the nursery. "What a fussy baby you have!" Out in public, a well-meaning person will say, "What a good baby. Is he always like this?" Such a question can put the mother in a bind. Although she may answer "yes," she may also remember that the previous week he cried all during a shopping trip.

One of the hardest times to deal with a crying infant is at night. After giving to your baby all day, you may feel drained and resentful when you have to give again at night. You may grit your teeth when awakened at 3 a.m. and feel overwhelmed. But if you can think of your baby as expressing needs, you may feel more accepting.

Once you understand that your baby's crying is a kind of communication, you may find yourself responding differently, trying to understand why he cries, or why he doesn't sleep as much as you think he should or as much as you would like. And you may also feel less harassed when your baby fusses in public. It's easier to be comfortable with him when you no longer feel pressured to have a "good" baby.

How long will my baby be anxious around strangers?

Your baby, until the age of six months or so, will usually be content with being held by relatives and family friends. She may even smile and play when you place her in someone else's arms. But between seven and nine months, she'll begin to resist people other than you and may cry when someone else is playful with her or reach for you when someone else tries to hold her. During this stage, your baby may even feel anxious about her grandparents and familiar babysitters.

Such reactions, which are a normal part of a baby's development, result from her growing awareness of the world. Your baby recognizes you as special and different, and views you with pleasure. Because she has good feelings about you, she wants to be with you and isn't as comfortable with other people.

Also, babies believe that something exists only as long as they can see it. Therefore, when you walk out of sight, your baby may feel anxious and cry. When she's back in your arms, she feels happy and safe.

This developmental stage can be difficult because it sometimes causes embarrassment and makes it hard to accept help with child care. A relative or friend, offering to care for your baby, may feel rejected by your baby's anxious cries. Some adults blame the parents, saying, "You've spoiled her by holding her so much!"

When your baby enters this developmental stage, it's helpful to remember that anxiety about strangers and separation is normal. It isn't necessary to force her to go to other people—she'll soon do that willingly. Just try to meet her needs, and if you need to, have others talk to her and play with her while you hold her. You can explain to people that, while you understand their feelings of frustration and rejection, you know that your baby is acting as most babies her age do.

During this stage, many babies have trouble separating from their parents at day care or when a babysitter comes. Explain the situation to your caregiver, and let her know that your baby may need extra holding and comforting. If your baby cries as you go, you also may find it hard to separate. Have your caregiver try to distract her. Call shortly after leaving to make sure that all is going well.

At times you might be tempted to leave while your baby is distracted and unaware that you're going. While this eliminates the initial rush of tears, she may react with surprise and fear when she discovers you've left. It's always better to say a quick good-bye. You'll know that your baby's fear of strangers and separation is lessening when you see her reach for someone other than you, and when you see her go happily to someone who's reaching for her. As this stage passes, she'll once again feel more comfortable and content with others.

Is it okay if my baby is attached to a blanket or other objects?

A young child clutching a blanket is a familiar sight. Between the ages of six and nine months, many babies become attached to a security object such as a blanket or stuffed animal. And the attachment may last until the child is four or five—or older. This is a natural part of development, although not all children pick out a special object, and some choose several soft items to hold onto. A child with a strong attachment may wake up clutching his blanket and hold it as his parents pick him up. He may put the blanket against his face and carry it around with him as he gets older.

To a young child, a blanket or other soft object is a source of warmth and comfort. He may use his "blankie" during times of transition throughout the day—when he goes to sleep, wakes up, feels tired or hurt, goes for a car trip, visits the doctor, or goes to day care—and during major changes in his life or routine. Such changes can include the birth of a sibling, the beginning of day care or nursery school, or a parent's absence. Children who are left to cry themselves to sleep may become particularly dependent on an object for comfort.

Your child's attachment to a special object may go through different stages. At times he'll have an intense need for his blanket and will let you know that he wants it, even if he can't yet tell you in words. At other times, during calm periods and as he gets older, he'll have less need for the special object.

If your child is attached to a special object, you may find it hard to trust that he'll ever give it up. You may wonder if you should remove it or wean him away from it, but as time goes on, your child's desire for the object will diminish, and he'll give it up on his own. However, you may not see this happen until he's five, since many four- and five-year-olds keep their objects with them at night as a source of comfort. Interestingly, when parents recognize how strong and long-lasting their child's attachment is, they sometimes begin to feel protective of the object themselves.

Should I give my child a pacifier?

A baby feels calm when her natural sucking instinct is satisfied. Some babies suck their thumbs, some nurse frequently, some suck on fingers or a blanket, and many use pacifiers. When parents first offer a pacifier to their child, they see how tranquil she becomes and how convenient the pacifier is to use. It's an easy, concrete, accessible way to soothe a crying baby. Parents can offer it in the car, leave it in the crib so their child can suck on it as she falls asleep, or, as she gets older, leave it near her toys so she can use it whenever she wants.

There's nothing wrong with a pacifier, and a child who uses one is not harmed. Yet, despite growing acceptance, some people believe pacifiers symbolize dependency and immaturity, especially when used by a child past infancy. A parent can easily feel under attack when told, "That thing looks awful hanging out of her mouth," or "She's much too old to use a pacifier."

Parents look to their pediatrician for advice and support on all aspects of childrearing, including pacifier use, but there are pediatricians who oppose pacifiers. One mother never let her child take her pacifier along on doctor visits because her pediatrician disapproved. It was easier for this mother to hide what she did rather than face ridicule or a challenge to her parenting beliefs.

Aside from dealing with outside criticism, many parents have their own doubts. When and how will their child ever give up such a comforting and satisfying object?

Children do give them up. Gradually, and in spite of the strong attachment you may now observe, your child will limit her use of the pacifier to times when she's tired or feeling stress. By age two, she may wean herself completely from it, or at least let you know, by rejecting it at times or accepting it less often, that she's ready to stop using it.

However, if you decide to take your child's pacifier away before she shows a willingness to give it up on her own, do so gradually over several weeks. If she's really not ready to give the pacifier up, she may begin sucking her thumb, blanket, or other object, so be prepared to offer substitutes such as juice, extra holding and cuddling, or gentle patting on her back as she goes off to sleep.

Why won't my child hold still during diaper changes?

A father walked out of his son's bedroom shaking his head. "I don't believe it. He only weighs twenty pounds and I still can't get him to hold still for a diaper change." Getting a baby diapered and dressed requires a surprising amount of skill and patience, even though the job is a short one. Toddlers, who are usually in constant motion, squirm and resist diaper changes. They're excited about their world, their interests change constantly, and they want to move and explore. Because they have a hard time putting off any of their urges, even for a moment, they don't like to lie still.

Distraction can sometimes make diapering a little easier. Put some toys or interesting playthings and objects nearby, and keep handing them to your child. This might occupy him during a quick change. You also can try singing to him or making interesting noises, but you may still have to restrain him a bit until you get him changed. You'll naturally feel frustrated as he resists and struggles, but just remember that your toddler has a strong drive to assert himself and explore and that's why he won't hold still.

How much childproofing should I do?

Childproofing your home is important because young children explore indiscriminately. If an object is within reach, a child under three or four will touch it without considering his own safety or the value of the object. Because young children have such a strong natural compulsion to touch, see, and explore, parents have to make the environment safe. But parents also have to balance their child-proofing with an understanding of their child's need to explore.

Parents know to put plugs in electrical sockets, to put locks on cabinets containing dangerous substances, to keep plants and sharp items out of reach, and to put away valuables. But beyond that, they wonder how much childproofing they should do. Some parents feel they should teach their child the meaning of "no" by leaving out objects that he's not allowed to handle: "Sooner or later, he's going to have to learn not to touch everything." Other parents leave out forbidden objects or refuse to let their child touch accessible items in order to train him to behave well in other people's homes. One mother who didn't want to let her son play behind the living room curtains, said, "I don't care about my own curtains but I'm afraid he'll play with the curtains at this friend's house." Such fears prevent many parents from allowing their child to explore his own house. Yet children can be allowed to touch and play with things at home and taught not to do the same thing at other people's homes.

Parents who leave out knickknacks and declare many items untouchable will find themselves in constant conflict with their child, who simply doesn't have the impulse control to resist touching. One common battleground is the kitchen. Frustrated parents who don't understand the developmental urge to explore understandably try to limit their child's access to the refrigerator, cabinets, and drawers. Yet such denial may only make a young child more frantic to experiment with things he sees his parents use. He may run to the kitchen every time he hears the refrigerator open, or he may try to climb on the dishwasher door when it's open. He just wants to touch and look, but parents often expect too much from a child under three and then feel drained by saying "no" all day.

How can I keep my child safe when he wants to explore?

It's certainly true that your child needs limits, but he also needs you to be understanding and patient with him. He'll probably be more cooperative if you show him what he wants to see and if you let him touch or explore (considering his safety) what he's interested in. He'll also inevitably learn his limitations because there are dangerous and valuable objects that can't be put away: a fireplace, lamps, a TV, a stereo. There's no need to intentionally leave out other forbidden things, just as there's no need to automatically declare all cabinets or things in your living room off-limits.

If your child has an interest in the dishwasher, for instance, you can put some spoons and plastic dishes and cups inside, within his reach, and let him occasionally practice taking them out and putting them back. Likewise, if you put some healthy snacks on the bottom shelf of the refrigerator, your child will probably feel satisfied helping himself to them without feeling a need to touch everything else in the refrigerator. If you're firm about not letting your child handle a few items, but otherwise allow him freedom to touch, you and your child will not be overly frustrated during this developmental stage. The more freedom he has, the more likely he'll be to listen when you tell him not to touch. Once you've fully childproofed your home, limiting the number of objects your child may not touch, you won't feel tense when he explores. However, expect to keep reminding him of his limits; he can't remember them well at this age, and his urge to touch is so strong that he may not be able to stop himself.

What should I do when my child touches things at other people's houses?

While you'll want to keep your child from handling things at someone else's house, you might find that your child is more cautious when he's away from home and that he does less exploring in other people's homes than you expected. When you visit others, you may need to do some temporary childproofing, especially if your host doesn't have young children. Ask if you can temporarily move fragile items. Most people will understand, particularly if you offer to put the objects back in place before you leave.

When will my child's desire to touch everything end?

Although it may seem to you that the touching phase will never end, you'll see a gradual decrease in your child's need to explore every-thing in sight. By the time he's four, he'll gain more understanding about objects, safety, and impulse control, and have less need to touch. You will then be able to put back on your tables and shelves many of the objects you had to keep out of reach. Childproofing is basically a way of accommodating the normal developmental needs of a child under three or four. Young children want to touch and try everything, so if you prepare for this stage, you'll have an easier time getting through it.

My child puts everything in her mouth. What can I do?

Babies don't just put things in their mouths for pleasure or comfort; they also use their mouths for exploration. They learn about objects by tasting them, feeling their texture, and experimenting with them. Until a child is about one and a half to two years old, many things that she plays with will eventually go into her mouth. She'll pick up things from the floor, chew on her stroller safety strap, and try to put her parents' keys in her mouth.

Because she can't tell what's safe or unsafe, you have to be very watchful. If your child is at this oral stage, you must pick up pieces of fuzz, crumbs, and small toys so she will not accidentally choke on them. You also have to be sure that the objects she puts in her mouth are clean and safe.

This developmental phase may seem long and tiresome to you, but if you start pulling safe objects out of your child's mouth or telling her, "Only food goes in your mouth," she'll get frustrated, and you'll be depriving her of pleasure and a chance to explore. Try instead to realize and accept the fact that she has to put objects in her mouth because that's a major way she learns about her environment.

When should I wean?

It's sometimes hard for parents to follow their young child's lead, especially when it comes to weaning. A child will nurse or use a bottle only as long as he needs to, but it can be hard to trust that a child will stop on his own. Parents sometimes try to hurry their child by taking away the bottle, breast, or pacifier before he's ready.

There's a lot of pressure on parents to wean their child. The pressure can be strong when a child reaches one year old and increases as he grows. Friends and relatives ask, "What's he doing with a bottle? Can't he drink from a cup yet?" The pediatrician may say, "He doesn't need to nurse or use a bottle anymore." Others may comment, "He's too big for a bottle." Negative remarks are directed not just at a child, but at the parents as well. "What's wrong with you? Why are you still nursing?" "Why don't you take his bottle away?" "He doesn't need a sippy cup anymore."

Parents feel especially self-conscious when judged by other parents. If parents of a two-year-old believe theirs is the only child on the playground who still drinks from a bottle, they'll wonder how it looks to other people and what other parents are thinking. They'll doubt their own judgment and wonder what they've done wrong or what's wrong with their child: "Do I baby him too much? Do we give in to him?"

If the bottle, breast, or pacifier is taken away from your child too soon, he'll probably look for other ways to satisfy his sucking needs. He might become irritable or start sucking his blanket. One mother, who threw out her fifteen-month-old's bottles on the advice of her pediatrician, said, "My son seems OK, but he started sucking his thumb." Some breast-fed babies who are weaned at twelve months may not yet be ready to give up sucking. If they're only offered a sippy cup, they may suck the top of the cup just as they would suck on a nipple.

If you feel the need to hurry the weaning process, you should do so carefully. The process should be stretched over several weeks so your child is not forced to abruptly give up something important. And remember that many toddlers and preschool children relax with a bottle or sippy cup before going to sleep.

As your child gives up the bottle or breast, you may have ambivalent feelings. If you nursed, you may feel good about "having your body to yourself" again, or you may be glad to stop fussing with bottles. But you also may feel sad to give up the warm, close feeling you had as you held your child and offered him milk or watched him lie contentedly with his bottle. You also may miss the free time you had when he drank quietly by himself. Whatever your feelings—impatience or reluctance—in time your child will be weaned. If you can wait until he is ready to wean himself, the process will be simpler and more natural.

Out of sight, out of mind—does every baby think this way?

Until a baby is eight or nine months old, he believes that objects and people exist only if he can see them. At six months, if you take a toy away from your baby and hide it behind your back as he watches, he'll act as though there no longer is a toy. In the same way, when you leave his side to go into another room, he may believe you no longer exist. Your disappearance upsets him, which explains the anxiety and tears you see.

When you play peek-a-boo with your baby, you reenact the anxiety and relief he feels each time you leave and return. You hide behind your hands or a blanket, and he believes you're no longer there. He may even become momentarily upset and whimper. When you suddenly reappear and say "peek-a-boo," he laughs with delight to have you back.

By nine or ten months, your baby will have some idea that objects exist even when he can't see them. At this age, he may look for a hidden toy if he sees you put it behind your back or under a pillow. But at times he may still react with fear and uncertainty when you leave him, because his understanding of people's permanence is not fully developed and won't be until he's between eighteen and twenty-four months old.

When will my baby begin to crawl?

Crawling is an important stage in development, and parents watch with delight as their baby becomes mobile. Although some babies start crawling before they're six months old, most begin between six and ten months, and some never crawl, going from sitting to walking without the middle step. Because children develop at their own pace, each baby will begin to crawl when she's ready. But if your baby has not begun by the time she's nine or ten months old, you may want to talk to your pediatrician about her motor development.

Some parents wonder if they can motivate their baby to crawl by putting toys just out of her reach. Rather than help, this may only frustrate her if she's not able to start moving. There's really no need to encourage crawling because babies have an innate desire to get to many different objects and explore their surroundings. As soon as she's developmentally ready and able to extend herself, she'll start crawling.

When your baby first begins to move, you may see her "belly crawl" across the floor. She'll move backwards or forwards, pulling with alternating arms while her belly stays flat on the floor. Later, she'll get up on all fours, rocking a little. Eventually, she'll move slowly on all fours, mastering the movement until she becomes a proficient crawler.

How can I keep my crawling baby safe?

Since a crawling baby will be able to reach many potentially dangerous objects, you'll have to babyproof your home, an often time-consuming and frustrating task. You should put plants, small toys, and fragile items out of reach, but you should not stifle your baby's natural curiosity about the objects she sees. As long as harmful items are out of the way, let her crawl to the curtains, touch the table leg, or reach for a toy. That's how she learns about her world. Of course, during this stage you'll need to keep your floors clear of fuzz, small objects, and crumbs that could end up in her mouth.

You'll naturally be concerned about stairs once your baby is mobile. The best way to be sure she's safe is to use gates at the top and bottom of the stairway. If you have carpeting on the steps and bottom landing, you may want to attach your gate a few steps up so your baby can crawl up and down the short distance safely. However, if your landing is not carpeted, you'll want to attach the gate to the bottom step to minimize harmful falls. She'll quickly learn to climb the stairs and will enjoy going up, but most children don't come down steps safely until they're one and a half to two years old. That's why it's so important to close the top gate each time you pass through. Once you've made your child's environment safe, you can relax and let her enjoy crawling.

When will my child start walking?

A child will begin to walk as soon as he's developmentally ready. For some children, that means at nine months; for others, eighteen months. The age at which a healthy child walks has no effect on or connection with his intelligence, yet parents often feel pressure if their child is a late walker. Friends and relatives may ask, "Are you sure he's all right? Why isn't he walking yet?" or say, "My daughter was walking when she was ten months old, and your child's already seventeen months," or "Maybe your son needs to be around other children so he can learn by watching them." Such comments cause parents needless anxiety, because there's nothing wrong with a developmentally healthy child who doesn't walk until he's eighteen months old.

There's no need to try and teach your child to walk. Although it might be fun for you to hold your child's hands and let him walk along, such an exercise will not help him walk alone any faster. Try to be patient and wait until he's ready for this stage of development.

He'll prepare for independent walking by first learning to pull himself up to a standing position while holding onto furniture. Once he's mastered this skill (which might take days, weeks, or even months), he'll begin to take steps while holding onto furniture or onto your hand. Eventually, he'll let go and take some steps alone. When your child starts walking, he'll be so delighted with himself that he'll hardly notice his frequent falls.

As your child begins to stand and walk, his perspective will change. Before, he looked at everything from ground level, but once he's upright, he'll see more. People, objects, and even his own body will look different. He'll be able to reach more things and to roam farther and faster, and that means you'll have to continue child-proofing his environment.

You'll find that one of the most delightful aspects of this developmental stage is your child's ability to go for walks with you. As soon as he's steady on his feet, take him for a leisurely walk outside. Walk at his pace, sometimes letting him choose the direction, and see how many wonderful discoveries he makes. He'll want to stop and examine pebbles, grass, worms, and flowers, and if you bring a collecting bag along, he can take some treasures home.

Is it frustrating to go places with a child who's learning to walk?

The more your toddler walks, the less he'll want to use his stroller, which can cause problems when you're in a hurry or when you're going far. If you're in a shopping center and want to encourage him to stay in his stroller, try distracting him with food or a toy. If this doesn't work, try to find an uncrowded spot where he can walk for a little while without bumping into people. Often, he'll want to push the stroller himself, and in a crowd this can cause quite a fuss. If you let him push for a little while, he may be more agreeable when you place him back in his stroller.

Although his slowness and desire to practice his new skill may temporarily frustrate you, you'll enjoy his excitement and independence. And you may be surprised to see that once he masters walking, he'll be just as likely to run as to walk.

Chapter 2 EATING AND SLEEPING

- Is it normal if my child won't fall asleep alone?
- Is it okay if I stay with my child at bedtime until she falls asleep?
- My child wants to sleep in our bed. Is this all right?
- If we let our child sleep with us, will we ever have the bed to ourselves?
- How often should my child be napping?
- When should my child sleep in a bed?
- Is there any way to make the transition from crib to bed easier?
- Why does my child drop food from his high chair?
- When should my child use a spoon and fork?
- Should my child at least taste new foods?
- Why did my child become a picky eater?
- How can I convince my child to try new foods?

Is it normal if my child won't fall asleep alone?

Yes, many parents have problems getting their young child to sleep at night. When it's time for bed, a young child often wants to be fed, held, walked, sung to, talked to, read to, or comforted. She wants her parents to spend time with her as she falls asleep, but they'd rather put her quickly and peacefully to bed, and then get on with their own activities.

You may wonder why your child won't fall asleep alone, especially when you hear, or imagine, that other children go to sleep easily. It's true that some children quickly fall asleep and that others are content to lie down with a bottle, sippy cup, pacifier, blanket, or stuffed animal. But most young children have a genuine need for their parents to be with them at night.

Bedtime can be a lonely, frightening time for young children, who naturally feel safer and more comfortable if their parents stay with them. Even three-, four-, and five-year-olds prefer not to be alone at night. One child said, "I can fall asleep better if you stay in my room," and another asked her parents, "Why do you want me to go to sleep? Don't you want to be with me?" A child finds it hard to understand her parents' need to be alone—she simply has no such need herself.

The intensity of a child's bedtime need for her parents can be judged by the struggles that occur when they leave her in her room. A baby might spend a long time crying, while an older child might get up or call out for water, another kiss, a trip to the bathroom, and anything else that would bring her parents close again. Elaborate bedtime rituals can take forty minutes or longer and often leave parents angry and frustrated. But what happens if, instead of spending forty minutes trying to get your child to fall asleep alone, you spend ten to twenty minutes keeping her company—feeding her or rubbing her back or lying next to her? She'll probably feel content and secure, and fall asleep peacefully without a bedtime struggle.

Is it okay if I stay with my child at bedtime until she falls asleep?

Once you see how strong your child's need and desire for closeness are, you may choose to stay with her at bedtime. In this situation, as in many others, you'll have to lower your expectations. While you'll have less free time, you'll also eliminate many nighttime problems associated with your child's loneliness, fear, and insecurity, and you'll help your child end the day in a calm and relaxed way.

If you decide to stay with your child until she falls asleep, you may find that few people you discuss the situation with will give you support and encouragement. Many parents do stay with their children, but few talk about it because they fear criticism. In a parent discussion group, one mother blurted out that her baby wouldn't fall asleep unless she was nursed. She expected to hear criticism, but instead saw other mothers at the meeting nod their heads. Their babies behaved the same way.

The time you spend helping your child fall asleep should be pleasant for both of you. You can use the time to relax, think, enjoy your child's closeness, or read. At times you'll probably nap or even fall asleep for the night. You may want to adjust your schedule to accommodate this by getting up earlier in the morning.

You may be afraid that if you stay with your child at bedtime, she'll become manipulative or unwilling to ever fall asleep alone. It's true that she'll get used to having you with her, but as she gets older, her need for your company at bedtime will lessen.

My child wants to sleep in our bed. Is this all right?

Your young child often needs you during the night. As an infant, he may wake up crying for you, and as a toddler he may call out for you or get out of bed to find you. Some parents meet their child's nighttime needs by going to their child's room and comforting him there. But other parents find it easier at times to let their child sleep in bed with them. They find that everyone sleeps better when they're all together.

The thought of a child sleeping with his parents shocks some people who've been conditioned to believe the experience is harmful. Many parents who let their child sleep with them at night are reluctant to discuss the issue because they think their situation is unique. Yet many parents have their children sleep in bed with them.

Young children end up in their parents' beds for a variety of reasons. Parents might bring their wakeful infant to bed so they can tend to him without having to get up during the night. Or they might want him near so they can be sure he's safe and so he can feel emotionally secure. Parents of a toddler may find their child climbing into bed with them on his own during the night. A toddler who's determined to be with his parents will climb out of his crib or bed and go to their room. One four-year-old told his parents, "I think of scary things in my bed, but when I get into your bed they go away." If parents won't let their child into their bed, their child might try to sleep on the floor next to their bed or in the hallway outside their door.

If you choose to let your child sleep in bed with you, you may still have concerns. You might wonder if you're being too responsive to your infant, toddler, or preschooler, or if your child will become too dependent on you. It's true that your child may develop a habit of sleeping in your bed, but he won't be harmed by this. Rather, he'll benefit from the reassurance and sense of security he receives from such closeness.

If we let our child sleep with us, will we ever have the bed to ourselves?

When parents start letting their child sleep with them, they may wonder if they'll ever again have a bed to themselves. Parents of a nine-month-old can feel overwhelmed by the thought that their child may be in bed with them for a few years, although actually, children's sleeping patterns and needs are hard to predict, and parents' expectations change as children develop. The amount of time a child will spend in his parents' bed varies between families and within families over time. Some parents have their infant with them for the first six months to a year. Some parents let their toddler or preschooler fall asleep in their bed and then move him to his own room each night; he may spend the whole night there or wake up and come back to his parents' room. Some children spend part of every night with their parents, while others come to their parents' bed only occasionally.

Some parents find that having their child in bed is not very restful. An infant makes many sounds as he sleeps, and a toddler or preschooler may toss and turn, waking his parents. Some pediatricians who are advocates of the family bed recommend that parents buy themselves a queen- or king-size bed so they can accommodate their child. Another possibility is for parents to place a mattress or crib in their room so their child can sleep nearby.

Most parents who let their child sleep in bed with them focus on the results. They often report that their child doesn't have nightmares and has fewer problems falling asleep when he's in bed with them. And families tend to get more sleep when parents don't have to wake up and go to their child in another room. Parents who are away from their child all day enjoy the chance to be close to him at night, to give a middle-of-the-night hug and say, "I love you."

If you're concerned about having your child in your bed, remember that there are different ways to meet his needs. If you're comfortable going to your child's room, that's a good choice for you. And if you prefer bringing your child back to your own room, that's also okay. Whichever way you choose to respond, the important thing is to give your child the security (even in the middle of the night) that comes with your attention, love, and care.

How often should my child be napping?

Each child has his own patterns of napping, which change as he grows. During the first months of infancy, your baby will spend much of the day sleeping and then, for the next six months to a year, nap in the morning and again in the afternoon.

By eighteen months, most toddlers take one nap. Many children stop napping by age two. Others nap until they're four. Some children don't take predictable naps, even in infancy. Some parents are flexible about naps and let their children follow their own natural sleep patterns, while other parents are advocates of strict scheduling.

A child's napping pattern may depend on the amount of sleep he gets at night. A child who sleeps ten hours at night will probably need an afternoon nap, while a child who sleeps twelve hours may not need to sleep again during the day. Toddlers typically sleep between ten and thirteen hours a night, depending on their nap schedules. By the time your child is two and a half or three years old, his napping might interfere with his nighttime sleeping, so that if he naps for a couple of hours he may be filled with energy at 10 or 11 p.m. This is fine if your schedule permits late-morning sleeping or if you like to spend the evening hours with your child. But if you want him to go to bed earlier, try keeping him from napping or at least from napping so long. Some parents are especially reluctant to let their child nap in the car, since a few minutes of sleeping there can take the place of a much longer nap at home.

Keeping your child from napping, however, can sometimes cause problems. Some children are very irritable when they don't sleep during the day, so you might decide that eliminating his nap is not worth the struggle. Your child might go to bed earlier if he doesn't nap, but if he's unhappy all afternoon and evening, your family hasn't gained much. Similarly, many children are tired and irritable if their nap is cut short, although some are able to wake up after a short nap feeling rested and ready to play.

Children in day care often nap as they would at home. Infants sleep when they need to, and older children, who are up early in the morning, generally nap for a couple of hours. These naps often keep children from going to sleep during the early evening hours, but they also allow parents extra time with their child. Parents can request that their preschool-aged child in day care not take a nap if it gets in the way of him going to bed at a reasonable hour.

Many babies only fall asleep for their naps after being fed. Toddlers who don't want to separate from their parents or end their play will often fall asleep with a short car ride, or after being rocked or patted to sleep.

If your child doesn't nap regularly, you may feel frustrated at the lack of time for yourself. But if you try to force him to nap, there will be negative consequences. He may spend long periods crying, and you'll probably become angry at him and at yourself for forcing the issue. It's never good to let your baby cry himself to sleep.

When should my child sleep in a bed?

Moving from a crib to a bed is a big change for a toddler or preschooler. After being in a crib, she'll now be able to control how she gets in and out of bed.

You may wonder what it'll be like when your child has her own bed. Will she fall out at night? Will she get out of bed frequently? Will she play and entertain herself in bed as she did in the crib? Will she feel comfortable and secure? And you might also have mixed feelings about your child's transition from crib to bed. It's exciting to watch your child grow, but it's also easy to feel nostalgic as she gets older.

One of the questions parents frequently ask is, "When will my child be old enough to sleep in a bed?" Some children move to a bed when they're as young as twenty months—usually because a new sibling needs the crib. But if the crib isn't needed, you can probably wait until your child is two and a half or three years old before making the switch. By that time, she may be ready for the move and excited by the idea of having her own bed.

Is there any way to make the transition from crib to bed easier?

The transition from crib to bed shouldn't come when your child is going through major changes, such as your return to work or the beginning of day care or nursery school. At these times, she'll probably need the security of her familiar crib. If the change to a bed is planned in anticipation of a new baby, try not to wait until your baby is born to make the switch, but rather give your child a month or so to get used to sleeping in a bed.

If your child is three and you're buying a new bed or sheets, you might want to take her shopping with you. Be careful about telling her that she's getting a bed because she's "big now." Young children feel a desire and pressure to be older, and sometimes the suggestion that they should act "big" adds stress to a situation, especially if there's a new baby in the family.

Once you have the bed, if there's room, try putting it next to her crib so she can make a gradual switch from one to the other. Your child can begin by taking naps in the bed, and then slowly start spending nights there. If she was used to having toys in her crib, put some on her bed. After a few weeks, when she no longer needs her crib, take it down, letting her help. Or, if you're going to use the crib for a new baby, your child might want to help you move it to the other room.

If you're concerned about your child's safety in a bed, buy a bed rail that will keep her from falling out. You also can put the box spring and mattress on the floor rather than on a frame so she can climb in and out of bed easily without getting hurt—and she can even jump on her bed safely this way. You might want to get your child a full-size mattress so you can cuddle up and read to her or, at times, sleep with her. Once she's moved from a crib to a bed, don't be surprised when she gets out of her bed in the middle of the night and comes to your room. Most young children feel safer and more comfortable sleeping in their parents' beds.

During this time of transition, notice how she feels about the change. If she's having a difficult time giving up her crib, slow down. Even if you planned to use the crib for a new baby, you can postpone the change by putting your newborn in a cradle or portable crib for several months. And when you do give the crib to your baby, don't be surprised if your older child still shows an interest in playing or sleeping in it. Children notice when babies get attention and occasionally like to pretend they're babies and go back to familiar objects and places. As long as your child doesn't feel pressure to give up her crib before she's ready, her transition to a bed should be smooth.

Why does my child drop food from his high chair?

Young children, especially between the ages of ten and eighteen months, tend to make messes when they eat. As they sit in their high chairs, they mash food, spread it around, and drop it on the floor—sometimes pea by pea, occasionally a bowlful at a time.

You may wonder why your child acts this way. Is he doing it to bother, defy, or manipulate you? Usually not. He might throw his food down because he's finished eating and doesn't want any more, or because he doesn't like the food he's been given. He might also just be tired and ready to get down from the high chair. Often, a child makes a mess because he's playing with his food, experimenting with the textures and spreading the food around to see what happens. A young child is interested in his meal not just for its taste but for its color and feel, and he doesn't mind getting messy in his explorations.

When a young child methodically drops bits of food onto the floor, he may be testing his own power over objects and his ability to make things happen. Children repeat this process because they seem to have a strong inner need to perform the same actions over and over. As a child drops his food, he feels delighted that he can control each piece, deciding where it will land and watching it fall.

To ease the cleanup, spread newspaper or a piece of vinyl under your child's high chair so you don't have to wipe the floor. And try putting less food on his tray. That way he'll still have a little to experiment with, while you'll have less to clean up. This phase, in which your child likes to drop things (toys as well as food), can be irritating. If he's at this developmental stage, you'll probably find that he won't listen when you tell him to stop. This happens because your young, egocentric child can't consider your wishes and his own at the same time. He ends up considering just his own desires and drops food—and toys—even when you tell him not to. If you can view this impersonally or even playfully, without thinking that he's trying to provoke you, you'll have an easier time dealing with him and simply picking the food and toys up.

When should my child use a spoon and fork?

Soon after your child begins sitting in a high chair, she'll probably want to try feeding herself. At first, she'll use her hands to pick up food, getting some in her hair, on her clothes, and on the floor.

Eventually, she'll become a bit neater and start eating with utensils, although she'll still use her hands sometimes.

Some parents are so bothered by messy eating that they try to stop their child from feeding herself. They think that meals will be faster and more efficient if they do the feeding, and they're probably right. Yet there are other considerations. Your child can become so frustrated when she isn't allowed to touch her food or feed herself that she might push away what you offer and even refuse to eat. All children at some point have a desire to feed themselves, and they're usually more cooperative at the table when their parents let them try.

When your child is ready to start feeding herself, you can minimize messiness by putting only a small amount of food on the tray (although some tolerant parents let their child plunge into a whole bowlful). When your child is ten to fourteen months old, you may see signs that she's ready to try a utensil. She might reach for the spoon you're using, or imitate your actions as you eat your meals or feed her.

Her first utensil should be a spoon, since it's safer to use than a fork. You can continue to feed her with your spoon while letting her dip her own spoon into the bowls of food. Between fourteen and eighteen months, she may be ready to use a child-sized fork, as long as you watch to see she doesn't harm herself.

Don't be concerned about the way your child holds her utensils; if she seems comfortable and is able to get some food into her mouth, there's no need to worry. If she seems uncomfortable, you can show her how to hold a spoon or fork correctly, but don't get into a struggle if she refuses to follow your example. Eventually she'll learn by imitating you.

If she doesn't want to use a utensil even though she's old enough and prefers eating with her hands, try to accept the situation. She may be more successful eating that way or may just prefer to touch her food directly. Since eating should be a relaxed and enjoyable experience, it's not wise to try forcing your young child to use a spoon and fork. Just have utensils available so she can try them out when she's ready. Between the ages of two and three, she'll be using utensils much of the time.

Should my child at least taste new foods?

All parents want mealtime to be pleasant, enjoyable, and healthy, and they want their children to eat a variety of foods. But often the ways in which they try to accomplish these goals are self-defeating.

Parents may put new food in front of their child and say, "Just taste it." They hope, of course, that he'll enjoy the food and therefore ask for more. They also hope that after trying one taste, he'll get used to experimenting with new foods. However, what often happens is that he refuses the taste, and a power struggle develops.

Parents sometimes try threats or various types of persuasion. "You won't get dessert unless you taste this." Using dessert as an incentive focuses too much attention on sweets and often causes a child to expect dessert as a reward. Parents also say, "But it's good for you," "It'll make you big and strong," and "Some poor children don't have any food to eat." But children ignore such statements, which are based in part on falsehoods. There's no instant strength from food, and eating a meal won't help another child who has to go without.

Although you may succeed in having your child taste something new, there can certainly be negative consequences. First, your child will seldom, if ever, ask for more of the rejected food. And if you're eating in public, his refusal to eat more than one bite can lead to embarrassment. One young child, forced to taste apple pie at a friend's party, declared loudly, "I hate this dessert!" Once a child decides he doesn't want what's offered, he usually won't change his mind. Another negative effect of forcing children to taste food is the risk of establishing a life-long pattern of aversion. Many adults continue to avoid food they remember being forced to eat when they were young.

Struggles over food are often as much about eating as they are about power. Children feel powerless when they're not able to say, "I don't want it." And when they do try a bite of something they don't want, they eat only because they feel they have no choice, or they want to please their parents, or they want dessert.

When your child resists food, he's usually not being stubborn. It's just hard for him to tolerate a taste he finds unpleasant. Often, he decides that he likes or doesn't like something based on its looks and consistency. Therefore, he may know at first sight that he doesn't want to try something new. Occasionally, he may refuse food because he's afraid that once he tries a bite, he'll have to keep on trying more and more new foods.

Yet, despite all the negative effects and emotions involved in forcing a taste, parents get into mealtime struggles for a positive reason: they want their children to eat nutritious foods willingly. And there are ways to accomplish this without resorting to arguments. You can talk to your pediatrician or a nutritionist about alternatives for healthy eating and consult books and online advice for recipes and meals that accommodate a range of tastes. Provide healthy snacks your child generally enjoys, and model for your child the kind of healthy eating habits you want him to adopt.

At mealtime, provide healthful food and leave him free to choose what he wants to eat. You'll find that when there's no coercion or arguing, meals will be more relaxed and your child will be more willing to try new foods. As your child gets older, his tastes will change, and he'll eat different types and amounts of food. For pleasant and healthy eating, the best thing to do is offer a variety of good food without putting on the pressure.

Why did my child become a picky eater?

"Sit there until you finish your peas." "If you don't have room for salad, you don't have room for dessert." "Just take three more bites." "If you don't eat what's on your plate, you won't get anything for the rest of the night."

Parents say and do all sorts of things to get their kids to eat. Some threaten, others bargain, and some make their child sit at the dinner table even after the rest of the family has left. As most parents find out, coercion doesn't cure a picky eater. Parents need only think back to their own childhoods. You were probably forced to try a food that was unappetizing or to finish eating when you were already full.

Picky eating is usually the result of stress and arguments about the quantity and variety of food. If your child has no control over what, when, and how much she eats, she'll feel powerless and frustrated—as any adult in the same situation would. Your child may angrily demand certain foods or react passively by picking at what's on her plate and taking tiny bites. In either case, she's not consciously trying to manipulate you, but rather acting out her sense of helplessness.

Picky eaters may avoid tastes and textures they find unappealing. They may also refuse to try new foods—perhaps they've been pressured too often to taste something different. A child who has faced frequent arguments about trying or finishing new foods finds it safer to stick to the few dishes she likes.

You may inadvertently create a picky eater if you pressure your child to eat large quantities of food or finish what's on her plate. A child with a small appetite can't help but feel upset if she's urged to eat more, and more often, than she wants.

When you coerce your child into eating, the results are usually negative. First, meals become unpleasant times of arguments and power struggles. Also, your child may resort to sneakiness, either stealing the foods she wants (usually sweets) or secretly disposing of foods she won't eat. Some children hide their unwanted food in their napkin and then throw the napkin away. One child managed to slide her peas behind the refrigerator. Another put bits of food on her brother's plate when he wasn't looking. And there are always children who feed their food to the family pet.

How can I convince my child to try new foods?

If your child's a picky eater, try removing mealtime pressure. Although your goal is to keep your child well-nourished and healthy, you shouldn't force her to eat. Children who willingly eat well-balanced meals and try a variety of foods have usually been fed with a low-stress approach. From an early age, they've been allowed to pick and choose, without pressure, from an assortment of foods. If you create such an atmosphere in your home now, your child's eating habits will likely improve.

Let your child determine how much she wants to eat. Since you have a realistic idea of her appetite, don't urge her to eat more than she usually does. She'll eat enough to keep from being hungry. If you believe she's underweight or exceptionally small, don't force her to eat extra food. Instead, discuss your concerns with your pediatrician, who may offer suggestions or otherwise reassure you.

You might try starting her day off with a nutritious milk shake. Put milk, fresh fruit, nonfat ice cream or yogurt, and protein powder in a blender, and whip into a frothy shake. And notice what foods your child's eaten over several days. If she eats less at one meal, she'll balance her intake by eating more later in the day. Before a growth spurt, your child's appetite may increase. And kids' appetites can vary from meal to meal and day to day.

Generally, prepare foods you know your child will eat, and don't pressure her to try new foods. Once she feels she can accept or reject something new without angering you, she may be more willing to taste what you offer.

Be careful not to humiliate or tease her about being a picky eater. If you let her know you accept her eating habits, she'll feel more relaxed at mealtimes. You may be embarrassed if she acts picky when eating at someone else's house, but you can help ease the pressure there, too. Usually, others will pay no attention to what she eats. If your host asks ahead of time, let her know that your child has a small appetite or eats only certain foods. Most people are understanding of children's needs.

If you eliminate mealtime stress and your child is still excessively picky, look deeper for reasons. She may feel overly controlled in other areas of her life and may try to exert some power by rejecting food. It's also possible that she'll remain a picky eater no matter what you do. Some people, including adults, are just very particular about food.

It takes patience to deal with a picky eater, but the rewards can be great. Once your child believes she has some control over what she eats, both she and you will feel calmer. Then, instead of focusing on what and how much she's eating, your family can concentrate on enjoying mealtimes together.

Chapter 3

THE TODDLER YEARS: ON THE GO

How different is the view from my child's level?

Toddlers scramble out of their strollers, climb on anything handy, and insist on being picked up because they want to see better and reach farther. When a child stands on the floor, he can't look out of most windows. Beds and toilets seem very high and big, and door-knobs and light switches are unreachable.

In public places, almost nothing is placed at a child's eye level. One mother walked into a health clinic and introduced her three-year-old son to the receptionist, who was sitting behind a high counter. The boy couldn't see anyone to say hello to and just stared at the wall in front of him until the woman peeked over to look at him.

When your child goes to a public bathroom, the toilets, sinks, towels, and dryers are all out of reach. Most water fountains are too high for him to use, and most of the interesting features of stores and restaurants—cash registers, cafeteria counters, bakery bins—are out of sight. When he has to sit in a stroller, his view is even more limited.

To see what your child sees, get down to his level and look around. You won't see your own kitchen sink or the tops of your tables. In a store, you won't be able to look at what people are doing behind counters or see most of the interesting merchandise. You'll notice that at nursery schools and day care centers everything is at eye level, and all the tables, chairs, and shelves are easy for children to reach.

Once you see how unsatisfying your child's view can be, you'll understand why he wants to climb and be carried. Pick him up often so he can see what's happening around him, and provide safe stools or pillows at home so he can climb a little and see more of his world.

How can I be prepared for falls and accidents?

Young children spend so much time running, climbing, and jumping that minor injuries are inevitable. Sometimes a child is so absorbed in play that she ignores her scrapes and goes right back to her game, perhaps after yelling, "You bumped me, you stupid chair." At other times, especially when she's tired, she may cry for a long time after a fall.

Your child's reaction to an injury often depends on who's around her. Since she feels most comfortable expressing her feelings to you, she might cry or complain more about a fall when you're with her. Many parents have seen their child fall, get up looking unhurt, and then start crying as soon as she sees them. A child cries like this because she wants to be comforted. When you're not close by, your child may comfort herself or seek help from another child or adult. Adults react the same way to their own injuries: when an adult bumps into something at home, where she's comfortable, she'll express her pain, but if she hurts herself away from home, she's likely to hide her discomfort.

The way a child reacts to a fall also depends on her age. A very young child is much more likely than a four- or five-year-old to cry after a minor injury. One five-year-old told her friend, "Just don't think about your cut, and it won't hurt anymore."

Many children want Band-Aids for every scrape and bruise. Band-Aids seem magical to a young child because she believes that once small cuts are covered up, they're gone. You can make Band-Aids easily accessible. Let your child wear one whenever she thinks she needs it, even if she just wants to cover an old scab she's rediscovered—the comfort is worth the small expense.

What should I do when my child gets hurt?

Just as children react in different ways to injuries, so do parents. Some minimize their child's pain and say, "You're okay. Stop crying." Others offer to rub or kiss the sore spot. Certainly children need comfort when they're upset after a fall, and they need to know their parents understand: "It really hurts when you scrape your knee." But children get hurt so frequently that it can be hard for parents to constantly comfort and reassure them. Yet some young children seem to need attention for each new cut, bump, or bruise.

Try not to overreact to your child's injuries. Some parents who usually realize they're overreacting but have trouble controlling their impulses, rush to their child after a fall, anxiously asking, "Are you all right?" When a child sees her parents looking so concerned, she may start to cry simply because she thinks something must be wrong. If parents continually overreact, their child may eventually feel that she's incapable of making herself feel better and that she should seek help for even minor accidents.

Some parents are very uncomfortable seeing their son cry after a fall. They may tell him, "You're a big boy, you can handle it. It's only a little cut." Even now, there are parents who think it's all right for girls, but not for boys, to cry. Parents should remember that young children of both sexes sometimes need comfort and sometimes need to handle minor injuries on their own.

When you watch your child playing, you probably warn her about dangerous situations. "Don't climb up there or you'll fall!" If she climbs and falls anyway, you may have a hard time being sympathetic. It's tempting to say, "I told you you'd get hurt if you played like that," but if your child is in need of comfort, she'll feel rejected by this statement and not understand the safety message you intend to pass on. In such a situation, you should pay attention to her pain while also telling her that what she did was unsafe.

On rare occasions, your child's injury may be serious enough for a trip to the doctor or the hospital. A serious accident is always frightening for parents and children, especially if there's a great deal of rushing and concern. If your child needs special treatment, reassure her. "I know your arm hurts, and I'm going to see what we can do to make you feel better. That's why we're going to the hospital."

Try to remain calm and explain (or ask the doctors or nurses to explain) the medical procedures to your child. Your child may not be able to avoid pain and unpleasantness in this situation, but you can be there to help her and go with her to the treatment room if permitted.

It's always hard to see your child in pain after an accident, and you might feel better if you bring someone along to help and comfort you—a friend, neighbor, or relative. As one mother said after her daughter received stitches, "I hear about this happening to other children, but it's very different when it happens to your own."

Is climbing normal?

After your child has been walking for a month or so, she'll probably start climbing on chairs, beds, couches, and anything else she can reach. She climbs because she has a strong urge to touch and explore things around her. When she sees you doing seemingly magical things, like talking on the phone, using the computer, washing dishes, turning on the lights, or opening doors, she wants to get closer and imitate you. And in order to do that—to reach the phone or the desktop—she has to climb.

The climbing stage can be difficult because you have to keep your child safe, and that can mean almost constant supervision. If you leave her alone for even a few moments, you may hear the sound of a chair scraping along as your child prepares for her next climb. You might stop her from climbing because you fear for her safety, because furniture might be damaged, or simply because you don't want her to climb. But her urge to climb is strong, and she may get angry and frustrated when she's held back.

A child who climbs during the day may climb out of her crib at night or at naptime, either to be with her parents or to explore the room. Parents often are surprised the first time this happens. One mother put her child in the crib for a nap, and then went to take a shower. As she was lathering her hair, she heard a noise in the bathroom and looked out to see her daughter standing there.

Once your child starts climbing out of her crib, she's probably ready to sleep in a bed. To keep her safe and satisfied during the day, try at times to make climbing easy for her. Take more trips to the park, where she can practice climbing with your supervision. You might want to give her a small step stool to carry around or get a small piece of indoor climbing equipment, such as a slide, for her to play on safely. You also can place a chair near a window so she can look out, take cushions off your couch so she can climb on them, or even put a mattress on the floor so she can climb, jump, and explore in safety.

Why does my child bite?

During infancy, babies find satisfaction in sucking and biting. Until about eighteen months, they bite and chew on toys, household objects, and other things they find in their explorations.

Sometimes your baby will bite because her gums are sore from teething. Although such a bite can be painful, you should remember that she's not intentionally trying to hurt you. Occasionally, a baby might bite while nursing. You may be so alarmed at this that you might wonder if you should start weaning, but such a drastic step isn't necessary. If you take the breast away from her and say "no" firmly, your baby will learn quickly.

An infant's innocent biting is very different from the deliberate, frustrated biting of a two-year-old. Sometimes a toddler's anger cannot be expressed through words, so, she may impulsively bite. Parents of toddlers who bite don't often feel understanding and accepting of the problem—and rightly so. When a child bites, parents should set firm limits, saying, "I don't want you biting anyone," or simply, "No biting." Letting her know immediately and firmly that biting is unacceptable is important. After you experience your child biting—just once—you need to increase your watchfulness. The more supervision you offer, the less likely it is that your child will have the chance to bite.

And since all children act out for a reason, try to figure out what's causing your child to bite. Are you spending enough fun and playful time with her? Does she watch you give a sibling more attention? Are your expectations reasonable for her young age? Are you arguing with your spouse in front of her? Are her days too scheduled? Are you setting enough—or too many—limits?

Occasionally you may be tempted to cure your child's biting by biting her back to "show her what it feels like." But biting a child back is wrong. First, you give a mixed message: you tell her not to bite, but then do it yourself. (Young children copy what their parents do.) Second, she's too young to put herself in another person's place and can't understand that the pain she feels from your bite is the same pain that she inflicts. You can teach appropriate behavior best by setting limits, spending a lot of time with her, helping her avoid too much frustration, and being a good role model for your child. And know that, at these young ages, children need constant reminders of how to behave in acceptable ways.

In stores my child wants to touch everything. How do I handle this?

Everyone likes to touch interesting and attractive objects. Adults in stores are drawn to gadgets they can manipulate and products they can pick up and feel. Children also want to handle what they see in stores, but many store owners and parents are too impatient or fearful to let children touch.

Touching is one of the main ways your child learns about

things around her, especially in new surroundings. Young children explore with their hands and often can only "see" something by feeling it. One three-year-old told her mother, who was holding an interesting object right in front of her daughter's eyes, "I can't see that far." The child was really saying that she wanted to touch it.

When children shop with their parents, struggles often develop as parents pick up, handle, and buy items, and children want to do the same. And because most stores try to display their products in the most attractive and appealing ways possible, the temptations for a child to touch are great. Parents usually keep their children from handling merchandise because they're worried about items getting broken. While it's true that young children don't understand the consequences of breaking things, it's also true that most children, if properly supervised, won't damage items in a store. Parents can hold fragile objects for close-up viewing or gentle touching, and can patiently allow their children, within limits, to pick up interesting merchandise.

Sometimes your child will be satisfied and more cooperative in a store if she's just given enough time to examine a few objects. Parents are often in too much of a hurry while shopping to wait while their child looks at boxes of paint brushes, shoes on display, toys on shelves, or piles of scarves. But many struggles can be avoided if you slow down a bit and allow an extra few minutes to accommodate your child by looking at what she's interested in. Your child is continuously receiving mini lessons in learning to value herself and her interests by the way you treat her.

Some stores make shopping easier by providing toys and play areas for children. If possible, patronize such stores and let the owners know that you value their service. Always support their efforts by watching your child while she's in the play area and by straightening up some of the toys before you leave the store.

Although play areas are very helpful, most of the stores you shop in will not have them, and many have little tolerance for children. Since that's the case, carry small toys from home when you shop with your child, or have her bring a backpack with her choice of a few small items. Such playthings may distract her from some, but not all, of the attractive merchandise around her. If parents, store owners, and employees recognized and became more patient with children's needs to see, touch and explore, shopping would become easier and more enjoyable for everyone.

Why do children have temper tantrums?

"I want this now!" shouts a two-year-old, pulling candy off the grocery shelf.

"Not today," says his mother.

When his mother refuses, he responds with a full-fledged temper tantrum: screaming, crying, thrashing, and kicking. Tantrums like this are hard to watch, they're embarrassing, and they can make parents feel helpless. They're also part of normal development.

Why do children have tantrums? At times a child is simply over-tired or hungry. Most often, however, the answers are rooted in developmental characteristics. Young children have very little self-control; they live in the here and now, and act on their immediate desires. When parents respond to their child's wishes by saying "no," he sometimes reacts negatively. Young children lack the ability to think logically and follow adult reasoning. A child will probably not understand why his parents deny one of his wishes, even though their explanations may make perfect sense to them. Another reason for temper tantrums, particularly with pre-verbal toddlers, is the young child's inability to express his needs and wants fully. When his parents can't understand him, he becomes easily frustrated.

How can I prevent my child's temper tantrums?

If you're concerned about temper tantrums, there are a number of approaches you can try, including prevention. Since you know your child's wants, you can guess which situations are likely to cause tantrums and plan ahead for these times. For example, when you anticipate a struggle at the candy counter or when shopping at a mall, carry a few small toys, some juice, or crackers with you. If the situation becomes tense, use these to distract your child. You also can set limits for your three- or four-year-old: "We're only looking today," or, "I'm only buying you one thing." But remember when you're in the store and your child sees something he wants, it'll be hard for him to remember your limits, and hard for him to "only look" and not buy.

It's also helpful to pay attention to your child's interests. Allow him to touch, look at, and explore things of interest, even if only for a few minutes. Under your supervision, allow your child to use the computer, take some food out of the refrigerator, pour the dog food into the bowl, water the plants, turn the light switch on, look around the hardware store, touch hanging belts in a store. This will help him feel a sense of satisfaction and he'll have fewer tantrums.

There's another technique that may prevent a tantrum: compromise. You can tell your child, "I won't buy candy, but I'll buy you a pretzel." This and the other prevention methods sometimes work well, but at times your child may have a temper tantrum in spite of your efforts. If this happens, you'll have to decide how to respond. Most likely your reaction will vary with the situation, depending on where you are and whom you're with. But your choices will be the same—you can meet your child's demand, distract him, or let him have the tantrum.

You may choose to meet his demand because you realize that it's not so unreasonable after all. Perhaps you were being too rigid when you first rejected his request. Or perhaps you feel that saying "no" is not worth the struggle or tantrum. If you give in, don't worry about whether your child will take advantage or remember that you gave in; your child reacts differently to each new moment and experience.

You can also try distracting him. Remind him about a recent pleasurable experience, point out something interesting, or talk about something fun that will happen soon. You may be surprised at how effective distraction can be in defusing a conflict.

Finally, you may end up choosing to let the tantrum run its course. Although coping can be hard, if you wait calmly and continue to try to distract him, your child will soon quiet down.

Tantrums are difficult for you and your young child. Once he outgrows that urgent need to have everything *now*, there will be far fewer tantrums to struggle with. Learning to deal with tantrums in a patient, reasonable manner that is respectful of your child's development, interests, and temperament, is good practice and can pave the way to smoother parenting and a happier, calmer child.

Why does my child keep saying, "I want to do it myself!"?

Young children want to try doing many things for themselves. An eighteen-month-old wants to push buttons, put a key in the keyhole, walk down the steps, and turn the light on. A two-year-old wants to assert his independence by pulling the wrapper off his candy, taking his shirt off, and putting a DVD in the player, while a three-year-old wants to put his shoes on, get his own vitamin out of the jar, use the computer, and pour his own juice. Sometimes children are successful at the tasks they choose for themselves, and at other times they struggle in frustration because they lack skills and dexterity. Still, the drive to do for themselves is very strong: "Don't help me!"

Parents who respect their child's desire to do things for himself help him develop a strong sense of autonomy. Since self-image is partly determined by the way you respond to your child's desire for independence, your child will feel good about himself when he's allowed to tackle jobs on his own. On the other hand, if you discourage your child too often, and do for him what he wants to do on his own or do for him what he's capable of doing, he'll begin to doubt his own abilities. When children doubt themselves during these years, it impacts their self-esteem during their elementary school years. Therefore, the message, "You're capable," needs to be strong during the early years.

In general, you should let your child at least start a task he's interested in. If he's unsuccessful, offer guidance, and if he's unable to follow your suggestions, offer to do the job for him. Don't jump in too soon because you find it difficult to watch your child struggle with a task. You may naturally want to help, but often your child doesn't want help. If you find it too hard to stay uninvolved, occupy yourself with something else while your child works.

What if my child insists on doing something himself, but he can't?

Sometimes you won't be able to let your child do a task for himself. One family was about to go home after seeing a circus when their two-year-old insisted on tying his own shoe. As his parents tried to help him and hurry him along, he became angry and frustrated, and nearby families stopped to watch the struggle. The parents finally solved the problem by telling their son he could carry his shoe out and tie it himself in the car, but often these conflicts are not easily resolved.

Despite your best intentions, you may find yourself in an embarrassing situation, carrying away your screaming, angry child who wants to stay put until he's finished a task. Such times are definitely hard, especially if you feel judged by others and frustrated by your child's actions. Yet your young child truly doesn't understand your feelings and will often focus only on his own needs and interests: "I want to do it myself!"

Sometimes you may not want your child to do a job for himself, because you know he can't really do it, because you don't want to deal with the mess that will result, or because you're in a hurry. But when you say, "Let me do that for you," you may be in for arguments, struggles, or temper tantrums.

To minimize such resistance, the best approach is distraction. "Why don't you look at this book while I put your shoes on?" As you button his shirt, talk about animals in the zoo. And while you're fastening his seatbelt tell him a story or start the DVD player you have in the car.

If a task your child wants to try is too difficult or messy, break it into steps, and let him try a small part of the job. If he can't yet brush his teeth, let him hold the toothbrush while you put the toothpaste on, and let him hold your hand as you brush. He'll feel pleased to participate, and in time, step-by-step, he'll take over the job for himself.

Being patient with children at this stage is difficult, because patience, distraction, and preparation don't always work—your child will angrily demand to do something for himself when you don't want him to or when he's incapable of doing the job. Still, the more he's allowed to try on his own, the less likely he is to argue when you have to take over a task. And as you see how pleased your child is with his accomplishments ("I did it!") and how good he feels about his abilities, you'll understand why it's important to let your child do many things for himself.

My daughter wants to dress herself. How do I handle this?

One of the first tasks most children try is getting dressed on their own. They feel proud and excited when they dress themselves, and they look to their parents for approval.

There's no need to try convincing or teaching your young child to dress herself because most children express an interest in the activity on their own. First, your child will learn to take off her shoes, socks, and pants, since children are able to take their clothes off before they can put them on. By age three, she may want to do most of her own dressing (excluding snaps and buttons), although her clothes will often be inside out or backwards. By the time she's four or five, she'll be able to dress herself completely with little help.

When your child begins dressing herself, she may be frustrated by zippers, snaps, buttons, and shirts with small neck openings. Even though she can't master these, she may insist on trying—a situation that often leads to anger and tantrums. You might want to avoid difficult clothes and buy pull-on pants and tops until she's ready to use fasteners.

As your child learns to dress herself, she may want to practice her new skills by changing her clothes several times a day, creating piles of clothing to clean up or launder. She also may want to choose her own clothes, sometimes picking the same easy-to-put-on outfit over and over, or choosing clothes that don't fit well, don't match, or are inappropriate for the weather or the occasion. As long as you're staying inside, there's no need to make an issue out of how she looks. But at times when you want her to look nice or dress appropriately for the weather, you may end up struggling over her choices.

What if I disagree with my child about what she wants to wear?

You can eliminate some of the problem by laying out two outfits and letting her choose one to wear, or by putting in her drawers only those clothes that fit and are suitable for the season. Another possibility is to fill one drawer with a few sets of clothes that mix and match, letting her choose what to wear from these preselected outfits. These suggestions require time and energy, but the effort might be worth it if your child is determined to pick out her own clothes each day.

When you're rushed, you may end up struggling with your child if she's determined to dress herself. If you leave the house every morning, you may be able to avoid arguments by setting the alarm clock fifteen minutes early to give her time to dress. At other times, let her know that you're going to help with dressing because you're in a rush. If she's generally been allowed to dress herself, she may not resist your efforts. But if she does, offer a distraction, "Let's get dressed quickly so you can pick out a CD to listen to in the car."

A surprising development may occur once your child has learned to dress herself efficiently: she may not want to do it anymore. She may say, "I can't," or "I don't want to," or "You get me dressed." Frequently, when a child has mastered a skill such as dressing, she sometimes loses interest, and it becomes a chore rather than a challenge. You may feel that if you give in and dress your child, you're being manipulated, or you may worry that she'll become too dependent on your help. You may even try to force her to dress herself, although when children are forced, they often slow down and procrastinate. You have to decide whether this is an issue worth struggling over.

Compromise and flexibility seem most effective. If your child is tired, uninterested, or simply wants to be taken care of for a while, it's all right to dress her yourself. At other times you may want to help her get dressed: "You do the shirt and I'll put on your pants." Most importantly, make the time you and your child spend together in the morning or while getting ready to go out pleasant.

It's best to avoid power struggles over getting dressed. In child development, steps forward are sometimes followed by steps backward. Enjoy your child's pride when she's able to dress herself, and trust that by age five or six she'll take on the job permanently.

When will my child be ready to use the toilet?

The transition from diapers to toilet use is an important one in your child's development. If you're patient and non-pressuring as he learns to use the toilet, you'll get through this stage fairly easily. But if you try to force toilet training or shame him when he has an accident, this stage may cause a lot of anger and unhappiness.

Parents sometimes initiate early toilet training because they feel a great deal of pressure. Nursery schools and day care centers want children to be trained, and friends and relatives offer criticism: "You were trained at two!" or "You really should start toilet training him." There's sometimes a feeling of competition among parents to see who has the youngest toilet-trained child, as though toilet training were a race. Many people mistakenly think that the faster a child develops (and the sooner he's toilet trained), the smarter or better he is.

Aside from starting toilet training in response to pressure, many parents start because they don't believe their child will learn on his own. Although they've seen their child learn to crawl and walk on his own, they find it hard to trust that he'll also use the toilet when he's ready.

Children can begin to use the toilet on their own, without urging from their parents, but the ages at which they're able to do so vary since, in this, as in all areas of development, some children are ready sooner than others. Between two and three, most gain enough bladder and bowel control to be able to use the toilet on their own, although some don't use the toilet routinely until they're three and a half. Emotional factors such as the birth of a sibling, a move, or a mother going back to work can delay a child's readiness.

Some children show an interest in the toilet at eighteen months, but you shouldn't take this as a sign that your toddler's ready for toilet training. At this age, your child's body is not mature enough, and any toilet use will be controlled by you. He's just temporarily interested in flushing the toilet, tearing toilet paper, and imitating you or his siblings. Some children under two or three are afraid of the toilet. It's large, and they fear they'll fall in or be flushed down. They may be afraid as they watch their bowel movement disappear. (Parents make a big deal over their child going in the toilet and then want to get rid of the results quickly!) A small potty seat is less frightening, but many children won't use one, insisting on the same toilet the rest of the family uses.

Is it possible to start toilet training too soon?

Yes, if parents initiate toilet training before their child is ready, the whole family may suffer. Parents use up a great deal of energy putting him on the toilet, constantly praising or showing disappointment, doing extra laundry and cleanup that results from frequent accidents, and working out reward systems using candy or stars to motivate their child. It's particularly difficult for parents to handle the resistance of a two-year-old who reacts negatively to any parental pressure or suggestions. At that age, a child strives for autonomy and wants to assert himself and take charge of many aspects of his life. It's best not to initiate toilet training when your child is at the "I wanna do it myself!" stage.

Many young children are not successfully trained if their parents start too soon. Efforts can backfire and a child can become strongly opposed to using the toilet. This situation can also develop if a child has been over-praised for toilet use, if he sees how (overly) important the issue is to his parents, or if he's been pressed too hard to be "a big boy."

Since praise can sometimes have negative consequences, give simple acknowledgment, help your child be aware of his own capabilities, and reflect back his pride and accomplishment, "You did it yourself!" You can relieve pressure your child may be feeling by being calm and matter-of-fact about toilet use: "Let's use the toilet before we go out." Offer support and help: "Can I turn the light on for you?" or "Do you need help with your pants?" Then don't comment on whether or not he used the toilet successfully.

Sometimes a child can feel so anxious about disappointing his parents that he won't even try using the toilet for fear of failure. Finally, a child who doesn't like to be pushed and controlled might try to exert his own power by rejecting his parents' suggestions. Rather than use the toilet, he might become constipated or go as soon as he's taken off the toilet, soiling the floor or his pants. If you feel you must initiate toilet training, hold off until your child is three, when it's developmentally easier to help him along, and make sure training doesn't interfere with other developmental changes.

However, the best approach is simply to wait until your child is ready to start on his own. Children have an innate drive to grow and develop, a strong desire to copy, imitate, and please their parents, and determination to do things for themselves. All of these urges will come together if your child isn't pressured to use the toilet before he's physically and emotionally ready. It takes a great deal of patience and confidence in your child to wait but eventually he'll let you know that he wants to use the toilet.

Once he's using the toilet, he'll occasionally have accidents because of stress or he'll forget to get to the bathroom on time because he's too busy playing. Your attitude toward toilet training determines, in large part, how successful this phase of your child's development will be. If you're relaxed and willing to let your child set the pace, you and he will have an easier time.

When will my child stop needing diapers (or Pull-Ups) at night?

There's a wide age range for toilet training, but by three or three and a half years old, most children have learned to use the toilet during the day. However, learning to stay dry at night sometimes takes a little longer, and many children occasionally wet at night until they're four or five years old. Nighttime control generally comes later than day control because a child must go for many hours without using a toilet before he's physiologically ready, and because a sleeping child can't consciously decide to go to the bathroom.

Your child may tell you that he wants to stop wearing diapers or Pull-Ups at night, or you may decide that he's ready because he's been consistently dry for many days. Sometimes a child who's dry at night will find it hard to give his diapers up, but if his parents put their child in Pull-Ups or let him know that diapers are available at night if he needs them, he'll probably switch to underpants without a problem. Once your child gives up diapers or Pull-Ups at night, don't be alarmed if he asks to go back to wearing a nighttime diaper or Pull-Up. Such a request is usually just a temporary desire to re-experience something familiar. If you allow him to try either of these again, in a short time he'll realize he doesn't need to wear them anymore. You might also distract him by talking about the different action figures or designs on his underpants.

Some parents choose to help their child stay dry at night by waking him up to use the bathroom, especially if he's had a lot to drink before bed. Other parents encourage their child to be a "big boy," although such urging misses the point. He'll be dry when he's mature enough and his body is ready. Pressuring a child to act older will not help and neither will shaming him or trying to make him feel guilty about wetting.

Even if your child has been dry for weeks or months, accidents are inevitable. If your child wets his bed, keep in mind that he's not doing it to frustrate or harass you. Either he's not quite ready to give up diapers or, if the accidents are occasional, he's sleeping too deeply to get himself to the bathroom. It's also possible that your child is reacting to the temporary stress of a move, a new baby in the family, or the start of school.

Whether your child has been having accidents or has not yet been dry enough to give up diapers or Pull-Ups, you probably feel impatient and frustrated. You may feel that he's been in diapers long enough or that you don't want to wash and change sheets frequently. These feelings are understandable, but once you realize that he'll be dry as soon as he's able, you can adjust your expectations and relax.

How do I find a good babysitter?

It can be difficult to find a babysitter you're comfortable using. When you leave your child for an afternoon or evening, you want to know that he'll be happy and safe. Yet it's hard to tell from a quick conversation or a few minutes' observation whether a sitter will be responsible. When parents can't turn to their parents or relatives for babysitting help, the best way to select a sitter is to ask for recommendations, get to know the sitter, and monitor carefully the way she performs the job.

To find potential sitters, ask friends, neighbors, relatives, and co-workers. You can also ask local high school teachers or counselors for suggestions. Good sources of names are sitters who may be too busy to work for you but who can pass on names of friends. Whatever your source for babysitters, get suggestions from people you trust. Also, as you seek referrals, keep in mind the ages of babysitters.

After you've contacted a potential sitter, invite her to your home so you can observe her with your child. Ask questions about her activities, schoolwork, and friends. She'll be pleased that you take an interest in her, and from her responses you'll get to know what she's like. Watch as she interacts with your child. Is she friendly, playful, nurturing? How does your child respond to her? One father was delighted when the girl he was interviewing spontaneously took out her keys and jiggled them in front of his whimpering eighteen-month-old, calming the child.

What instructions should I give to a new babysitter?

Ask the sitter to arrive early on the day she'll watch your child so you can give her instructions. If you hire a teenager, keep in mind that they need strong guidance and limits, so be prepared to tell your sitter in detail what your expectations are. Describe how you want her to handle feeding, playtime, television, the computer, toilet use, and bedtime, and write down your instructions so she can refer to them later. Make it clear if you don't want her to talk on the phone, text her friends, or take your child outside.

Before you leave, let your sitter know how you can be reached, and leave emergency phone numbers. You might also want to write down a list of activities your child enjoys and another list of things to do (take out play dough, put on a show, read books) if he gets silly or hard to handle. A four- or five-year-old may spend time testing a new sitter and feel a sense of power: "This is my house, my food, my TV." Let your child know ahead of time that you expect him to behave appropriately, and let your sitter know that it may take time for your child to feel comfortable with her.

If your child has a difficult time separating from you, you might feel tempted to leave without warning him or saying goodbye. But if you do this, you'll probably increase your child's anxiety. It's better to tell your child that you're going and have the sitter comfort him as you leave. If he'll be asleep when you go, tell him before bedtime, "While you're sleeping, Kim will come and babysit for you." You can also take time before the babysitter arrives to tell your child about the fun he'll have. If you let the sitter do special things with him—give an extra dessert, play a new game—he may be less anxious about your leaving.

If you want to check on a relatively new sitter, come home earlier than you said you would. And always ask how the afternoon or evening went. Since some sitters are reluctant to tell about difficulties or minor accidents, ask, "Any problems, scrapes, or bruises?"

Trust your instincts. If you feel that something happened while you were away, try to find out about it. If your child seems unhappy with a sitter, try to learn why. You can ask a three- to five-year-old, "What do you like about Michelle? What don't you like?" Although you may hear some exaggerated stories, take him seriously when he says, "She yells too much," or "She tries to scare us." If you're unsure about a sitter, ask a neighbor or relative to come by, and check next time the sitter's at your house. And if you feel that a sitter is not responsible, stop using her and look for someone else. In order to enjoy your time away from home, you have to feel good about the person watching your child.

Now my child needs me; now she doesn't. What's going on?

Parents are puzzled when their toddler, between twelve and twenty-four months, shifts from being dependent to being independent and back again. Why, for example, would she suddenly dart away from her mother and then just as suddenly come running back to her?

Such on-and-off behavior comes from your toddler's mixed feelings about her place in the world. When she first learns to walk, she develops a sense of independence and joy. She's delighted with her new-found skill and control, feeling that the world is at her command. Soon after exercising her new independence, however (sometime between seventeen months and two years), her perceptions of her place in the world change, and she can feel vulnerable. It's her joy in exploration combined with her feelings of uncertainty that lead her to run off and run back.

Typical of a toddler at this stage is an eighteen-month-old girl waiting in line with her mother at the post office. She wiggles away and goes to look at a chain hanging across a doorway. As soon as she reaches the chain she says, "Mommy, Mommy," and runs to get picked up. After a few seconds, she gets back down, runs and touches the chain, and then runs back to her mother. She repeats this cycle as long as she and her mother wait in line.

This developmental phase of emotional dependence-independence, which is a normal part of growth, can last until your child is two years old. Different children show different degrees of dependence. Some aren't comfortable exploring their surroundings on their own and may cling to their parents. Most children need more reassurance when they're out of their secure and comfortable homes.

During this stage, your toddler may be especially sensitive to your responses and easily upset when you disapprove of her behavior, just as she's pleased when you approve. Over time, as your young child gains more experience, a change will occur, and she'll be able to play, explore, and move about without coming to you for repeated reassurance. Until then, try to accept her behavior, smile, and wave when she goes off a bit on her own, and give her the emotional support she needs to feel secure about her world.

Why does my child always like to be where I am?

When they're at home, young children want to be near their parents. While the intensity of need varies with age and personality, between the ages of fifteen months and three years, your child may be more content playing and exploring when you're close by.

Young children like to be with their parents much of the time, day and night. Often, parents find that their child has an easier time falling asleep if they stay with him, patting his back or keeping him company. In the uneasy moments before sleep, he gains comfort when they're near.

Your child's desire to be with you is normal, and the attention he receives from you is essential for his development. As he comes to understand that you're there even when he can't see you, and that every time you go away you come back, your child will begin to feel secure and trusting.

Waiting for that to occur, however, can be frustrating, especially when you're followed by your child, who won't let you out of his sight. And at times, if your child stays close to you in public or when other adults are visiting, it can be an embarrassment.

Your baby will indicate his need for closeness by reaching out to be picked up. When he can crawl, he'll follow your voice and crawl to be near you. Later as a toddler, he'll often carry his toys from room to room to be with you. And although at three or four years old your child may spend time at preschool, day care, or a neighbor's house, he'll still prefer to be near you for your attention and involvement when he's home.

When your child wants to be with you, try to be understanding and accommodate him when possible, knowing that this stage of development is normal. Create spaces and things for him to do in different rooms in your home so that he can happily play near you.

When you have adult guests over, try to anticipate your child's need for attention. Suggest he draw pictures for the visitors to take home. Place some interesting toys next to your seat so he can play nearby. Such diversions may work, but it's unrealistic to expect him to leave you entirely alone. If you exclude your child, he may become demanding, silly, or whiny. But if you partially include him, focusing attention on him at least some of the time, you should be able to talk to your guests without too much interruption. This phase, like many other phases young children go through, is easy to handle with a little patience and understanding.

Why does my child say, "Only Mommy do it"?

Between the ages of twenty months and three years, some children won't let their fathers help them. When a father tries to comfort his child during the night, get her dressed, get her some juice, or even fasten her seat belt, she resists: "No! Only Mommy do it." Young children are often strongly attached to their mothers, and during this brief developmental phase they sometimes reject their fathers' help.

This stage can be frustrating. A father who wants to take an active role in caring for his child may find it hard to understand his young child's resistance and rejection. At times he may feel like giving up and telling his wife, "You take care of her. Why should I even try?" His feelings may be hurt, and he may show signs of resentment towards his child.

The mother's role, too, is difficult during this stage. It's hard for her to see her husband rejected and hard to try to persuade her child to allow him to help. There's also more pressure on the mother to take over the work of child care. This means she's always the one to get up at night, give comfort, and get the child ready in the morning.

One mother no sooner got into bed after feeding her two-month-old baby, when her three-year-old daughter called out for water. The tired mother asked her husband to respond, but their daughter refused his help. "Not you. I want water from Mommy." To avoid a middle-of-the-night struggle, the mother got up, but the encounter was unpleasant for both parents.

Some parents try reasoning with their child ("Mommy's tired") or forcing her to accept her father's help: "If you want a drink, you'll have to let Daddy get it." Sometimes these statements work, but sometimes tears and tantrums follow. It may be easier to give in, at least during the night, and have the mother get the drink so the family can go quickly back to sleep rather than deal with a struggle.

If the father's unable to help his child because she rejects him, he can still help his wife by taking over additional household responsibilities or caring for the couple's other children. And both parents should try not to let the father's feelings of rejection interfere with their relationship with their child. In the course of development, the stage of "only Mommy do it" is rather short.

Should I say, "You're a big boy now"?

Parents often can be heard telling their young child to act more maturely: "You're a big boy now, so you should use the toilet," or "You're too big to make such a mess." Parents use "big boy" as a discipline tool and as a way to change their child's behavior, either by appealing to his desire to do what older children do or by shaming him with a comparison to younger children.

The problem with urging your child to be a "big boy" is that your child, who already wants to act older and more capable, feels pressure to change and do things he may not be able to do. When he can't act like a "big boy," he may feel bad about parts of himself that he usually can't control and about not being able to please you. In a public restroom, a mother changed her son's diaper while telling him, "You're a big boy now. You're too old for diapers." He looked ashamed. Yet, if he had been ready to use the toilet, he would have given up diapers on his own. Exhortations to be "bigger" won't help your child—they'll only make him feel bad about himself.

In a similar situation, a woman took her grandson to a toy store and asked him to pick something out. When he chose a stuffed animal, she said, "Oh, no. Not that. You're too big to want that." When adults say such things, they tell a child that his feelings and desires are unacceptable, and that he should be acting differently.

If you think your child is not as "big" as he should be, try to understand why. He might use baby talk or play with a younger child's toys because of a new sibling, the start of day care or nursery school, or simply to get more attention. And since each child develops at his own pace, your child may just not be physically ready for the behavior changes you'd like to see. By temperament, he may be a child who cries more than other children or who needs more closeness and security. Also, children struggle as they grow, and for every step forward, there's sometimes a short step backward to earlier behavior.

All children have a strong drive to be independent and imitate older people. If you accept your child as he is and wait patiently without pressuring him, you'll see him begin to act "bigger" on his own.

What toys will my toddler like?
Twelve to Eighteen Months
Your child will enjoy trucks or cars he can sit on, push-and-pull toys, doll carriages, plastic lawn mowers, wheelbarrows, a two-step kitchen stool he can stand on to see high places, pounding boards, toy phones, music boxes, rocking toys, outside and indoor climbing equipment with short ladders and slides, and adults' shoes he can

walk around in. He'll also like simple toys he can take apart and plastic bottles with tops to take off and put on. And he'll like plastic containers, measuring cups, and paper cups.

Eighteen to Twenty-Four Months
Your child will enjoy stringing large wooden beads, screwing and unscrewing bottle caps, using a punching bag, pushing a toy shopping cart, using plastic tools, playing with balls of different sizes and shapes, arranging magnets on the refrigerator, and playing with stuffed animals. He may be happy for long periods playing with sand or water if he has shovels, pails, measuring cups, sieves, funnels, and plastic bottles to use. Although he will not be able to pedal yet, he may enjoy a toddler bike.

Two to Three Years
A child this age may enjoy rubber, plastic, or wooden animals, dolls and dolls' accessories; a play stove, refrigerator, and sink with dishes, pots, and pans; dress-up clothes; a play house; a doctor's kit; large blocks; cars and trucks; a play fire house and fire engine; and a toy garage and gas station. Most two- and three-year-olds (when supervised) can use pens, paint, crayons, chalk (fun to use on the sidewalk), big paint brushes to use with water outside, and, when closely supervised, child-size scissors. Your child will probably have fun jumping on a mattress that's flat on the floor, kicking a deflated ball that can't roll away from him, and riding a tricycle. He'll also like using puzzles, playing musical instruments, using the computer, and listening to CDs of folk, classical, or children's music.

When you provide toys for a child of any age, avoid giving too many that limit creative play. So many toys can only be put together and used in one way, and if your child spends all his time with such toys, he'll have little chance to make his own creations. Instead look for toys that can be used in a variety of ways, and ones that allow your child to use his imagination. For example, instead of buying kits of shrinkable plastic with pre-drawn pictures, buy the same plastic, without the drawings, at a craft store. Then your child can make his own designs.

As you buy toys, you may find that your child becomes intensely interested in a new plaything for several weeks and then loses interest. This is common, although it may be disturbing if you've spent time and energy shopping for the right toy, one your child said he "wanted so badly." Your child loses interest for several reasons: he may have quickly exhausted all the toy's play possibilities, he may have mastered the toy, figuring out how it works, or he may be frustrated because it isn't made well or is difficult to use.

To get more use from your child's discarded but almost new toys, put them away in a closet for several months. When you take them out, they'll seem unfamiliar to your child, and he may become interested in them again. He may even think of new ways to play with them, since his interests and his play are always changing.

And a child with an older sibling will get an early introduction to toys intended for older children. As your child grows, he'll let you know which toys interest him and which activities he wishes to pursue.

Are playgroups a good thing?

Parents probably benefit from playgroups more than their children do. Parents of very young children often feel isolated, so they welcome a chance to meet with other adults, compare child-rearing stories and advice, and observe how other parents handle their children. Of course, children also benefit from a playgroup, and as they get older, they enjoy seeing their friends regularly and playing at each other's homes.

Play—and a lot of it—is important in a child's life. It's one of the key ways children learn. An environment that fosters play, allowing a child's interests and imagination to grow is ideal—and hard to find. This is why playgroups can be so beneficial. And while parents typically use the time to socialize with adults, they can learn a lot about child development, and their child, by observing the group at play.

If you're interested in starting a playgroup, talk to other parents about the possibility. Although playgroups are most convenient when families live near each other, groups often form between people in different neighborhoods.

You can join or start a playgroup with your baby, knowing that you'll be the one to get the benefit. You'll be with your baby while you interact on a regular basis with other adults. You'll enjoy talking, exchanging ideas, and commiserating, and you'll probably find a lot of comfort in relating to the same questions about babies.

If you're joining or starting a playgroup with your toddler, consider that playgroups often work best with three to five children of mixed ages. If all the children are twenty months, there will be a great many issues over sharing, but if some of the children are two and some are three, group get-togethers will be more harmonious. The youngest child will be happy playing alone next to the others, and the oldest ones will be more likely than the two-year-olds to share toys.

What's a typical playgroup like?

During playgroup, your child might want your constant attention, saying, "Look at this," "Let's play with this," or "Watch me." While this can be frustrating, don't get upset with your child for behaving this way, even if you don't observe this in the other children. You might consider rejoining the playgroup at a later time. It's okay if a playgroup doesn't work out for you or your child.

Many playgroups are successful meeting in the morning, usually for an hour to an hour and a half, although some meet in the late afternoon, normally a slow time for at-home parents with young children. Other playgroups meet on the weekends so parents who work full time can participate.

Your playgroup will probably get together once a week, meeting at each member's house in turn. In some groups, every parent comes every time, while in others, parents rotate attendance so that in a group with four children, two parents attend any one session while two have the time free. The success of this rotating method depends on the ages and personalities of the children, and how well the families know each other. Some young children don't want to be separated from their parents.

Before your playgroup begins meeting, get together with the other parents involved, and develop rules and standards for practical issues. What kind of snacks will be served? What happens when children fight? Who should bring toys? How will you handle the problem of sharing?

Your playgroup will be most successful if your group shares similar interests and attitudes, especially regarding parenting, since conflicts can arise when one group member accepts behavior that bothers another. As long as the adults are compatible, you should be able to talk about differences and work out solutions to problems that come up.

Why is my child fascinated by the telephone?

Children like to do what their parents do, and parents spend a lot of time on the phone. Even before your child is two, he'll imitate you by using a toy phone, holding your cell phone, pushing the buttons, and making sounds. When your child is between eighteen months and two years, he'll want to talk on the phone and, given the chance, he's likely to listen and nod without saying a word. He's also likely to hold objects up to the phone so the listener can see them, since he assumes that if he can see something, everyone else can. One three-year-old had his aunt hold on while he got his pet hamster. "See," he said, holding the animal up to the receiver, "He's moving around."

Children like to imitate their parents by being first to answer the phone. Parents who want to avoid this situation shout, "I'll get it," but sometimes their child races to the phone also shouting, "I'll get it!" When a two-year-old answers the phone, he might just hold it, saying nothing. A three-year-old might pick up the phone and say, "Who's this?" and a four- or five-year-old who's given a message by a caller will probably forget it.

At these young ages, children's conversations are all about themselves. Once they've said what they want to say, they may simply hang up without thinking about the person on the other end. Young children do this because, at these egocentric ages, they can only think about their interests. "I have new shoes." "I'm eating ice cream." "Can you come over and play with me?" They can't think about what you're doing or ask with sincerity, "How are you?" They don't understand the give and take of conversations—and may not, until they're close to seven!

What should I do when my child interrupts my phone calls because he wants to talk too?

Your child is fascinated by the phone not only because you use it, but also because it has a magical quality. It's both tool and toy, and it lets your child share his thoughts with other people, something children like to do. If you're having a conversation, your young child will interrupt because he can't easily hold on to his thoughts. Be patient when he interrupts. This behavior is to be expected at these young ages. Don't say, "Can't you see I'm on the phone!"

Developmentally, young children can't consider their needs and someone else's needs at the same time. It's much easier to ask an adult to hold on than it is to ask a child to wait to be heard. If you worry that tending to your child during these interruptions will lead to a lack of manners, it won't. When you respond to these moments with politeness towards your child, he'll (gradually) learn to treat others politely. If he's ignored or yelled at, he'll learn to treat others in that way.

You might be frustrated when your child wants to talk, especially when you're on an important call. Your child might continuously say, "I want to talk," which can be embarrassing. If your child is too disruptive, you might have to end an important call, hoping the person on the other end will be understanding. Although you can gradually teach your five-year-old not to interrupt important calls, explanations do little good with younger, egocentric children. You can try distracting by offering toys or food, but don't be surprised if the interruptions continue.

One way you can accommodate your child's desire to answer the phone is to ask relatives or friends to call at prearranged times; then you can safely let your child answer and talk. If you're having a phone conversation with the parent of a child the same age as yours, ask if your child can talk for a few moments. Remind yourself when you need to that most callers are tolerant and understand a young child's interest in answering or talking on the phone.

Chapter 4

THE PRESCHOOL YEARS: DISCIPLINE

- How can I get my child to cooperate in the morning?
- My child sucks his thumb. Should I stop him?
- Why does my child want me with him at birthday parties?
- Why does my child act differently when she's away from me?
- How important is discipline and punishment?
- What styles of discipline work best with young children?
- Does spanking really help?
- How should I act when I am disciplining my child?
- When will disciplining my child get easier?
- What can I do about my child's whining?
- Am I spoiling my child?
- How should I react when my child says, "I hate you, Mommy"?
- Do I have to be consistent when setting limits?
- Can too much praise backfire?
- Is it okay to bribe children?
- Why does my child make such a mess?
- Should I make my child clean up?

How can I get my child to cooperate in the morning?

"Hurry up!" "I don't want to be late!" "You need to put your shoes on NOW!" Parents say these things over and over while they prepare breakfast, pack lunches, and help their child get ready for day care, school, a playdate, doctor's appointment, or an outing. In the midst of all this activity, young children dawdle along, seemingly unaware of the frustration they cause. It can seem to parents that nothing keeps their child from procrastinating—not logical arguments, threats, rewards, or punishments.

Most children need constant reminders. "Brush your teeth." "Put your coat on." "Stop playing." "Eat your breakfast." "Get your backpack." This is because they aren't interested in rushing off. Getting ready is something they have to do, but it's not a priority. They'd much rather get involved in playing, drawing, reading, using the computer, or watching TV. In addition, children have only a loose sense of time. Ten minutes can feel like plenty of time to finish playing and get dressed. It's parents, not children, who think time and morning routines are important.

Here are some strategies to try if you, like so many parents, have a child who doesn't cooperate in the morning. Try waking yourself up fifteen to twenty minutes earlier so your preparations won't be as hurried. With a little more time in the morning, you can relax, share a cup of cocoa with your child, talk during breakfast, maybe take a short walk. Even five minutes of relaxed time together can make the morning smoother. You can also wake your child up earlier so he has time to play before getting ready.

You might find mornings more peaceful if you make lunches, lay out clothes, and help your child pack up his backpack in the evening. What works for one family or child may not work for another. You may have tried many techniques and still find your mornings difficult. In that case, changing your attitude toward your child may help some. Instead of expecting him to take care of himself completely, accept that you'll have to help him along. It'll be faster and more peaceful for you to help your child get ready than to yell, "We're in a hurry!" Identify tasks he has the most trouble with and either offer help, do them for him, or keep calmly reminding him; all kids need constant reminders. He'll be more cooperative if you help him get dressed, talk to him while he brushes his teeth, or sit with him at the breakfast table. Don't nag your child about eating breakfast if he isn't ready or hungry. Instead, take sliced fruit, dry cereal, crackers, toast, and juice boxes in the car.

Don't worry about whether your assistance will hinder your child's ability or desire to become independent. The drive to become independent is so strong within children, there's no stopping it, no matter how helpful you are. There may even be a bonus; your child may learn, by your example, to be more patient, helpful, and kind.

The tone you set in the morning is what your child will take with him as he starts his day. If you're angry and frustrated, it'll be hard for him to start his day in a happy way. If you're calm and understanding, he'll have an easy time starting his day off with good feelings. If you change your expectations, you'll realize that your child is simply acting as most young children do. Instead of thinking about your child being uncooperative, help him get ready in a loving, fun, and calm way. It's important for both you and your child to start the day on a positive note.

My child sucks his thumb. Should I stop him?

Parent's reactions vary when their child starts sucking his thumb. Some feel strongly that it's good for him to fulfill his own needs this way, while others feel just as strongly that it's not. Because of the differing opinions, parents are sometimes unsure about what to do.

Babies begin sucking their thumbs for the same reasons they use pacifiers and frequent nursing or bottle drinking—to satisfy their sucking needs. The thumb is always there and so the child is always in control, which is not the case with the pacifier, breast, or bottle. And a baby who sucks his thumb may be less dependent on his parents to calm and soothe him since, with his thumb, he's able at times to comfort himself.

There are pediatricians who advocate thumb-sucking and even encourage new parents to help their baby get started on the habit as a natural and easy way for him to satisfy himself. Other doctors say that a baby who's given the breast or bottle on demand will already have his sucking needs met and will not need or desire his thumb. Of course, some pediatricians (and dentists) are against thumb-sucking, believing it's an unnecessary habit that may harm a child's teeth, especially if thumb-sucking continues beyond age four or five.

Just as pediatricians offer various opinions, parents, too, have different feelings about thumb-sucking. Many are unconcerned but do feel bothered by negative comments they hear from others. Friends, relatives, and even strangers will criticize a child for thumb-sucking and try to pressure his parents to stop him. For many families, this is the only problem connected with the habit.

In other families, thumb-sucking is looked on with ambivalence. Parents worry about their child's teeth, about how long he'll continue, about how he'll finally give it up, and about whether they should try to make him stop. And there are parents who don't want their child to suck his thumb at all and wonder about how to stop him right away.

If you notice this habit during the early months, try to feed more frequently, which may satisfy your baby's sucking needs. Otherwise, simply accept thumb-sucking as a natural habit. Trying to force your child to quit can have negative consequences and is usually unsuccessful because a thumb, unlike a pacifier, can't be taken away. If you pull your child's thumb out of his mouth, he'll most likely suck his thumb again as soon as he can.

Since sucking provides comfort, the more pressure you put on your child to stop, the more attached and dependent on his thumb he may become. Fearing ridicule and feeling vulnerable, your child may depend more and more on his thumb for comfort. Be patient and try not to discourage your child from thumb-sucking, at least through his preschool years.

Why does my child want me with him at birthday parties?

When a birthday invitation arrives in the mail, children are excited. They ask, "Can I go? When is it?" and talk eagerly about presents, cake, and goodie bags. But when the first excitement is over, your child may ask you another question: "Will you stay with me at the party?"

For some children, attending a party is difficult. A child may only want to go to a birthday party if his parents come along, and he may cling and ask them not to leave once he's arrived. This can happen even when the birthday child is a close friend and the birthday home or place is familiar.

A child who's shy or quiet in groups may prefer to observe at parties rather than participate and may only feel comfortable doing this when his parents are with him. He also may want them around because he feels temporarily overwhelmed by the excitement, the number of people at the party, unfamiliar fathers, or the unusual appearance of a friend's house decorated for a birthday. He may also be afraid if there are characters or a clown. If the party is in an unfamiliar place, he may feel even more unsure.

Whatever the reason for your child's reluctance to attend a party without you, it's understandable for you to feel frustrated. You may wonder why your child needs to be with you when other children the same age seem willing to stay at parties by themselves. And you might worry about your child's ability to interact with other children or his lack of independence.

If you recall your own childhood experiences at parties, you may feel more tolerant and accepting of your child's behavior. Most of us have mixed memories. We may have been happy about the cake and ice cream and games, but we also remember some disappointments and feelings of shyness and embarrassment.

If your child is anxious about attending a party, you can look for ways to make him feel more comfortable. For example, see if a close friend or neighbor is invited to the same party so they can go together. Being with a friend may make separating from you easier.

However, if he wants you to stay, try not to view it as a problem. Instead, enjoy the party, and let your child see you having fun rather than being annoyed. If you stay, your child will probably enjoy himself, and you and he can talk about the fun you both had at the party. And if you don't complain to other parents or bring the situation to their attention, and just act matter-of-fact about staying with your child, they either won't notice or will admire your patience and involvement!

Why does my child act differently when she's away from me?

When parents hear how well-behaved their child is with a relative, teacher, friend, or caretaker, their response is often, "That's not how she acts when she's with me." And conversely, when parents hear that their usually energetic child seemed withdrawn while spending time away from home, they wonder, "Why does she act differently when she's away from me?"

A child's behavior does change, depending on whom she's with and where she is. Parents see this when they pick their child up from school, day care, or a friend's house. As soon as they arrive, she may start acting negatively—whining, making demands, and clinging. When a parent asks if she's acted this way all along, the usual answer is, "No, she was fine until you got here." Parents may be partly relieved to hear their child enjoyed herself, but also partly upset and confused by her actions.

Most often, your child's behavior changes when you arrive because she's more comfortable when you're around. Once she sees you, she can express feelings she may have been keeping to herself. Perhaps her day was frustrating because she couldn't play with a favorite toy or felt pressure from her teacher, or because another child told her, "You're not my friend anymore." Or perhaps she was angry at you for leaving her with a caregiver. The day's frustrations all come out when you come to pick her up.

It's natural for your child to feel less comfortable expressing her needs and feelings when she's away from home. Adults, too, are more reserved when at work or in the company of others. Therefore, it's not surprising that a child who seems content all day will let off steam when she's with her parents.

Some young children are only comfortable playing and exploring when their parents are around. Once parents arrive to pick their child up, she may start playing and resist going home. A child in this position probably spent part of her day watching other kids engaged in activities she was interested in and now, with her parents in sight, she's eager to play. Therefore, some children don't really begin to enjoy themselves until it's time to leave.

If your child seems fussy after a day away from you or starts complaining when it's time to go home, be sure to question the teacher, friend, or caregiver. Ask about your child's interest and activity level, and try to get a true picture of her day.

If you know that her mood will change when she sees you, you can plan ahead. If she's whining, try to distract her. "When we get home, I'm going to get the play dough out." Or "I'm going to have a snack with you." And if you know she'll want to start playing when you're ready to pick her up from school or day care, arrive a little early or stay a little longer. That way, she'll have time to explore comfortably and then leave in a pleasant way.

How important is discipline and punishment?

Parents often feel they spend a great part of each day disciplining their young children: "Don't use the toy that way—you might hurt someone," "No hitting," "Leave the dog alone," "You have to come in now," "That's too loud," or "You need to listen better." Setting limits for young children can be difficult, frustrating, complex, and time-consuming, but it's essential. Parents have to teach their child acceptable behavior while controlling or changing unacceptable behavior until she's old enough to exert some self-control (by age three) and understand why rules are important (by age seven). In order to handle this task effectively, parents need information about their child's egocentric development, plus realistic expectations, empathy, patience, love, and respect for their child.

Disciplining young children is an extremely important part of parenting. Parents who don't set adequate limits do their child a great disservice. They also reinforce unacceptable behavior as their child quickly learns she can act as she wants.

Some parents feel overwhelmed by their child's behavior and may not know where to start. Other parents just don't think about the importance of setting limits or leave the job to friends, relatives, and most commonly, teachers. One reason parents fail to discipline their child is because they fear her anger, and they don't want to disappoint their child. Rather than face rejection or anger, they ignore unacceptable behavior, give in, or rationalize, "Kids will be kids."

But setting limits is one of the major responsibilities of parenting and is not a job that should be ignored or put off.

Many parents doubt their ability: "Am I too strict? Lenient? Do I expect too much?" Parents are embarrassed by their child's misbehavior in public and wonder what they've done wrong or why she seems worse than others. Since a child's behavior is often a reflection of her parents, they feel vulnerable and judged by others when their child acts inappropriately; such feelings are normal. Yet parents should realize that limits are very important, and misbehavior is a basic part of childhood. A child learns what is correct by trying all sorts of behavior, "good/right" and "bad/wrong," until she finds out what is and isn't acceptable.

Parents should base their expectations and methods of disciplining on their child's age and ability to understand. Distinguishing right from wrong is a gradual process, and young children don't yet have the necessary reasoning skills to fully understand right from wrong. In general, most children under five are motivated to change their behavior "because mommy said" or when threatened with a punishment, not because they understand how their negative behavior impacts others or fully understand right from wrong. The motivation to not hit comes from wanting to watch cartoons, play outside, or have dessert—not from thinking about someone else's feelings. It's normal for young children to reason in this way.

What styles of discipline work best with young children?

A child under two simply needs constant watching. He can be distracted rather than reasoned with. Saying "no, no" to issues of safety is the beginning of limit setting.

Children between the ages of two and three have such strong developmental needs to explore, touch, and do things for themselves that they have difficulty sticking to limits. Because their immediate needs are so great and because they focus so completely on the here and now, they usually don't realize they're doing something wrong, even if they've been told many times. When reprimanded, children this age often will look surprised and hurt.

In order to set limits for these young ages, parents (or caregivers) have to stay fairly close by, offer frequent reminders, get involved with the child, and always be aware of what she's doing. When children aren't supervised, they lose sight of acceptable and unacceptable behavior. If a child is playing inappropriately, her parents have to be right there to remove her from the situation and then involve her in something else. "You can play here on the cushions." Offering an alternative often works because young children can be easily distracted by interesting objects and activities.

Children three and under often reject limits and say "no," not only because they want to continue their activities, but because they're asserting their independence and learning what they can do. And sometimes parents set limits unnecessarily because they underestimate what a young child can do. A three-year-old who wanted to hold a screwdriver was told, "No, it's too sharp." But when she protested, her father decided to let her try as long as she sat next to him so he could supervise. She was happy, and her father realized that he could relax some of the limitations he'd set.

When a four- or five-year-old misbehaves, parents may momentarily withdraw their love and attention. Since a child wants parental approval, she feels hurt when she's criticized for doing something wrong. She can't separate her action from herself and feels that she's being rejected for who she is, not for what she has done. The removal of parental acceptance sometimes motivates a four- or five-year-old to change her behavior and to run to her parents for a hug after she's been disciplined.

Verbal limit-setting and distraction work with four- and five-year-olds, but since they have a better understanding of consequences than younger children do, they also respond to other methods of disciplining. Connecting a restriction to an activity works because a four- or five-year-old can understand the relationship: "If you want to ride your bike, you have to stay in front of the house," or "If you want to play outside, you have to keep your jacket on."

However, it's not always possible to find a connection. If a child hits her brother, what should her parents take away? Parents sometimes remove something unrelated, such as a toy, privilege, or dessert. Although it's unwise to make dessert a focus of power, many parents find that their child changes her behavior when threatened with the loss of sweets for a meal. She does this not because she understands her parents' point, but because she wants to avoid the punishment.

When taking something away or using any other form of discipline, parents should be sure the consequences come soon after the misbehavior. This gives the child a chance to connect her actions with their consequences, and it ensures that parents will follow through. Often, when parents tell a child in the morning that she'll be punished in the evening, she knows that they may forget or change their minds.

One mother, eating lunch in a fast food restaurant with her five-year-old, said, "If you keep misbehaving you're going to bed at 7:00 tonight." When the child continued acting up, the mother said, "All right. Now you're going to bed at 6:30." The punishment seemed so far away and so drastic to the child that she felt helpless and continued misbehaving. Instead of making a distant threat, the mother could have tried distracting her daughter, firmly telling her what to stop doing or warning her they'd have to leave the restaurant. Then the child could have made the connection between her behavior and the consequences.

A disciplining method that some parents find successful with three- to five-year-olds is counting: "By the time I count to five, I want you indoors," or "I'll count to ten while you get ready for your bath." This actually works well because it offers a limit, a warning, and a bit of time, although if the technique is overused it becomes ineffective.

Sometimes (but not always) "time-outs" work. However, if a "time-out" doesn't help your child change her behavior, don't use this method. If parents use "time-out," they can tell their child she can get off the step or chair when she's ready to play nicely. "Time-out" should only last as long as is necessary for her to calm down and change her behavior.

When a four- or five-year-old becomes angry and aggressive, her parents can set limits, change the situation, or try to distract her. If she doesn't calm down, they should firmly say, "You may not do this!" Along with a firm tone, it's okay to give THAT LOOK that conveys, "I mean it!" Gradually, a stern look and a slow shake of your head should deter your child from negative behavior.

Does spanking really help?

Parents may spank or hit their child in anger or frustration or when they don't know how else to get their point across. Some parents believe that spanking is the only way to teach their child to listen and behave well. Yet spanking is not necessary; there are other, more effective ways to get children to change their behavior.

In our society, spanking is still a widely accepted method of discipline. Many parents defend spanking by saying, "I was spanked and I turned out okay," or "It's the only way to get the message across." Others feel defensive and embarrassed about hitting their children: "I know I shouldn't have spanked him, but ..." Some parents feel guilty after spanking and want to follow up with a hug or an apology to assure themselves they haven't lost their child's love. Still other parents say that, though they spank, they really don't believe spanking changes their child's negative behavior. Even those parents who strongly believe in the effectiveness of spanking say it usually only temporarily stops inappropriate behavior.

There are problems with spanking. Most importantly, your child will imitate what you do. One three-year-old, after hitting her brother, was yelled at by her father: "Don't you ever hit your brother!" The three-year-old responded, "You did it. Last night you hit me." If you hit your child, why shouldn't she also hit when someone does something she doesn't like? Can you fairly tell your child not to hit when you discipline her by spanking? Does it make sense to tell your child to "use words" when she's angry, while you spank her when you're upset with her behavior?

Spanking can be a particular problem because a young child doesn't understand ahead of time that an action is wrong. If she's spanked, she won't easily see that she's done something inappropriate, but rather will focus on the pain and embarrassment of the spanking. It's very difficult for a young child to make a connection between her own behavior and a spanking, yet one of the goals of discipline is to have children make those connections.

Spanking a child may actually hinder discipline. All parents want their child to eventually develop self-discipline and a sense of right and wrong. As children grow older, they start to feel badly about their unacceptable behavior, and their gradually emerging sense of guilt keeps them from misbehaving as frequently. But when a child is spanked for her wrongdoings, she doesn't learn to monitor her own behavior. She may learn instead that, as long as she doesn't get caught, she can misbehave. And if she does get caught, guilty feelings she has will be relieved by the spanking, since she has paid the consequences. She'll learn that if she can tolerate the spanking, she doesn't have to feel bad about her negative actions or try to change her behavior. Even when parents explain to their child why they've spanked her and how they want her to change, she may be too angry or humiliated at the time of the spanking to listen and learn.

Discipline works best when you set firm limits verbally and then follow through by removing your child from the scene of her misbehavior, taking away an object or privilege she's abused, or having her spend time sitting away from the family until she changes her behavior. When punishment is relevant to the inappropriate behavior—when your child throws a block and is made to stop playing with the blocks—she learns to make the connection between her actions and its consequences. Until children develop self-control, they're motivated best by their desire for parental approval and the fear of losing privileges and toys.

Parents often think that they must spank their young child to teach critical safety rules, such as not to run in the street. Of course, making certain children are safe is a must. To keep children safe, parents need to closely supervise, and give consistent warnings and frequent reminders.

Sometimes parents say, "When I tell my child to stop, she ignores me, but when I spank her, she does what I want." One mother who was browsing in a department store with her three-year-old became angry when her daughter tried to investigate the dressing rooms. She repeatedly told her child not to go near them and then spanked her for not listening. The child cried, turned around in circles several times, and looked defeated. The situation is a familiar one, yet the mother had other options that would have left her and her child feeling happier. Since young children have a hard time listening to limits when they have an intense need to explore, the mother could have acknowledged her child's interest and even taken a moment to look into the dressing room with her. This might have made it easier for her child to do what she wanted.

Because children's behavior can be so frustrating, parents sometimes find themselves on the verge of "losing it" and may feel ready to hit or spank their child. At such times, it's important to remember that young children have only a limited ability to integrate rules.

Disciplining children is a necessary, complex, and gradual task. Your young child needs to be reminded of limits over and over, and often firmly. Try to have realistic and age-appropriate expectations, and be patient as she slowly learns self-discipline. If you spank her, she'll feel defenseless, humiliated, and angry, and won't understand the connection between what she did and what you're doing to her. It takes self-control not to spank and to trust that your child can still learn appropriate behavior.

How should I act when I am disciplining my child?

An important element of disciplining a child of any age is the tone of voice parents use. When they sound firm and sure of themselves, children often respond well, but when parents are unsure about what limits to impose, their children get mixed messages. The most effective tone is respectful but firm. Parents should begin setting a limit by speaking in a quiet, polite, firm voice. If that doesn't work, they can assert themselves more forcefully and speak in an authoritative voice. But yelling at a child is not as effective as firmly stating a limit (although it's often difficult to keep from yelling). It's sometimes helpful to stand close to a child, quietly repeating a warning or prohibition.

When disciplining a child, parents should always consider their own anger. Sometimes, when bothered by personal problems, parents may overreact to their child's behavior. Of course, parents should not be too forceful and harsh when disciplining their child. If the child always loses or is often given negative feedback and doesn't feel accepted, what incentive does she have to behave well?

Parents who are too hard on their child only encourage her anger and aggression while causing her to feel badly about herself.

It may be helpful for parents to remember their own feelings as children. Were they disciplined harshly? Do they want their child to know the same anger and frustration they once experienced? Parents who felt unfairly disciplined often say they won't treat their child the same way, but in moments of anger, it takes a great deal of patience to deal with misbehavior in appropriate ways.

Remember that children learn not just from your words, but from your actions. If you treat your child with kindness and respect and show that you value her, she'll model her behavior after yours. When children feel good, they usually behave nicely and have an easier time accepting the limits you impose. And when children are treated courteously, they learn what courteous behavior is. It's as important to praise and encourage your child when you're pleased with her as it is to set limits when you're unhappy.

As you discipline your child, you should look for the source of her misbehavior; otherwise, you'll spend time treating the symptoms rather than the cause of the problem. You may see dramatic changes in behavior when you give your child more time and positive attention or when you address situations that are troubling for her: a difficult school year, problems with friends, or uneasy sibling relationships.

When will disciplining my child get easier?

Disciplining is a difficult job that gets a little easier when children reach the early elementary years. At these ages, they've integrated many of the rules they've heard over and over, and they usually behave in socially acceptable ways, needing fewer reminders. Their impulsive exploration slows down and they give more thought to what they're doing. They also become more capable of listening to reason. Parents of an early-elementary-aged child reasonably expect her to consider other people's feelings, behave well in public, give of herself, and share with others.

Many adults use the same disciplinary methods their own parents used. "I was spanked, and I turned out okay." While teaching children right from wrong is essential, don't follow the examples of your past if they include spanking or slapping.

Effective discipline is neither harsh nor lenient. Harsh punishment, including spanking and other physical punishment, makes children angry and resentful. They aren't motivated to change their behavior, only to sneak and manipulate and try to get away with more misbehavior. They'll think about the unfairness of the punishment rather than their own actions. At the other extreme, discipline that's too lenient is ineffective. A chronically misbehaving child who only has to say a fast "I'm sorry" or tolerate a brief "time-out" won't learn to control her misbehavior.

Kids may misbehave because they want more attention paid to their words, interests, and activities. A child who feels left out or unconnected—perhaps because of family problems, a new baby at home, sibling rivalry, or a mother's return to work—may seek negative attention if that's all she can get. For example, one sibling may fight frequently with her brother because she feels he gets more of their parents' time. Then her anger and jealousy might be directed at him.

Sometimes children act out their frustration and sense of helplessness by misbehaving because they're unhappy, insecure, or unsuccessful in school. In such a situation, parents should talk with the teacher, offer more encouragement, and closely monitor their child's progress and behavior.

Be flexible and give encouragement and praise to reinforce positive actions. If you worry about how her behavior is viewed by other adults, take comfort in the fact that kids who misbehave at home often don't misbehave when they're out. More struggles take place between parent and child than between child and peers or child and other adults. A child who says, "You're mean!" to her parents usually knows it's unacceptable to say that to her teacher or her friends' parents. All people act and express themselves differently in the comfort of their homes.

Discipline is a difficult issue. If you're concerned about your child's behavior or unsure of your own ability to set limits, take parenting classes on discipline or consult with a professional who understands child development. Such specialists can help guide you in the appropriate direction.

What can I do about my child's whining?

Hearing a child whine is very annoying. Young children often whine when they're tired, hungry, angry, or frustrated, and once they start, it's difficult to stop them. When parents ignore their whining child, he usually just continues until they finally speak to him. And even those parents who try to be patient or who believe it's best not to focus on a whining child, often end up shouting, "Stop whining!" or "What did I tell you about whining! Use a grown-up voice!"

There are no easy ways to keep your child from whining. You can try redirecting his attention, although your attempts at distraction may be unsuccessful. You can also try letting him know that you're unhappy with his tone. But, when you say, "You're whining!" or "Stop whining!" you imply blame. Instead, try expressing your feelings in a less negative way, without using the word "whining" at all. Say, "You'll have to ask me in another way."

Sometimes, particularly if your child is three and a half or younger, you won't be able to understand what he says when he whines. You can tell him, "Ask me in a voice I can understand." You may not be able to stop your child's whining until you discover what's causing it. Sometimes a child with an older sibling whines because he feels he can't compete with his brother or sister. He turns to whining in order to be noticed. Sometimes children whine when they're tired, frustrated, or want something they think they won't get: "I want more ice cream."

By the time your child is four, he should be better able to express himself and understand the limits you place on his whining. "You'll have to find another way to tell me what you want." If he whines continuously, despite your efforts, he may believe whining is the best way to get what he wants. Try not to get too upset and annoyed by this typical behavior. Instead make changes in the way you respond to him. You may need to set more limits, listen to him more, and give him more time and positive attention.

Am I spoiling my child?

"You don't need that." "You already have one of those." "Stop asking for things." Young children can easily seem as if they're "spoiled." But it's important to remember that children don't understand what things cost, they can't value things the way you wish them to, and they don't look at what they already have and decide, "I have enough." Children under the ages of four and five are really too young to think in this way. More commonly, children ask for things ("I want a scooter") and expect more ("I want that. I saw it on TV.").

All young children occasionally act in selfish, spoiled ways. Children under five or six years old are developmentally self-centered and focused on their own desires, possessions, and activities. They often make demands without consideration for people or circumstances. "Why can't I have Barbie with the beach clothes now?" "I don't want to help." Their interests also shift. "I don't want to play with that anymore."

However, if your child constantly gets her way, she'll gradually learn to feel entitled to do as she wishes. This can happen if you don't set limits on her behavior or if you fail to follow through when she acts in unacceptable ways.

Many children are overindulged with material objects. Yet, owning many toys does not necessarily make a child spoiled; children with lots of possessions can be loving and considerate. However, if you constantly give without reinforcing positive values, you may unconsciously encourage your child to behave in socially unacceptable ways.

Some parents have a hard time controlling their buying. They may enjoy giving to their child or feel that buying presents is a great way to make their child happy. Some parents give out of guilt—they may not offer their child the time and attention she needs, so they buy gifts instead. Even when parents know they're overindulging their child, they may rationalize their actions. "She's only a kid for a short time." "Why not? We can afford it."

The danger in continually overindulging your child is that she might come to expect it. She may grow up unable to handle disappointment or tolerate situations that don't go her way. Since you want your child to become a caring, strong person, capable of taking care of herself, you need to set limits on her negative behavior, act as a positive role model, and show her by example how to graciously accept and offer kindness, and how to deal with disappointment. In the meantime, expect your child to say, "I want" over and over again and to frequently ask, "Can I get this?" Be patient with this stage, and give positive attention to what she's interested in: "Look at all those colors." "It moves fast." Just because you show interest in something doesn't mean you have to buy it. If she grows up with limits and these basic values, she won't act spoiled, no matter how many possessions she has.

How should I react when my child says, "I hate you, Mommy"?

When your young child gets angry with you, she may shout, "I hate you. You're dumb!" This outburst might come after you've said she can't go outdoors or have a friend over or do something else she wants to do. A preschooler has a hard time putting her exact feelings into words. She doesn't know how to say, "Daddy, I think you should let me stay up later tonight because..." or "I'm angry with you because you said..." She's too young for such articulation and too young to show that kind of respect. Instead she expresses her feelings and anger by saying, "I hate you."

Some parents accept and understand these words as the beginning of their child's expression of angry, negative feelings. But all parents can feel betrayed when their child, after receiving love and attention, turns on them over a minor disappointment. It can be frustrating when adult reasoning, logic, and caring fail to keep a child from yelling, "You mean Mom!"

Parents may be tolerant of a three-year-old yelling, "You dumb Mom!" but it's harder to be understanding when a four- or five-year-old says, "I hate you." A child's words can feel threatening to parents who don't like their children to be angry with them. And parents worry that a bad habit could develop.

It is common for parents who hear "I hate you" to say to their child, "That's not nice! Don't let me hear those words again." But a child needs to release her angry feelings somehow, and if she isn't allowed to express them verbally, she'll find other, perhaps more destructive ways. She might turn to aggressive behavior such as hitting, or she might take out her anger by becoming deliberately slow, acting excessively silly, or pretending she doesn't hear her parents. However, if her angry feelings are acknowledged and allowed to be expressed, she'll eventually learn to state her feelings more appropriately.

If your child says, "I hate you," offer her other ways to tell you how she feels. Suggest she say, "I'm mad at you," or "I'm angry," or "I don't like what you did." Acknowledge her feelings, but say, "I want you to tell me in different words."

And remember, children are natural mimics. Your child uses the word "hate" because she hears it so often. Adults say, "I hate this dress," "I hate when it rains," or "I hate it when people do that." It's natural for your child to use the word to express her dislike of something or someone, or to point out when you've said the word: "Aw, you said hate." You can take advantage of the fact that she's a mimic, stop using the word hate, and gradually teach your child to express her anger in acceptable ways.

When your child says, "I hate you," rather than make an issue of the words, simply restate her words and feelings. Say back to her, "You're really angry at me, aren't you? You don't like it when I say it's time to come in." If she hears you express her anger and disappointments in this way, she'll gradually begin to use similar statements herself.

Do I have to be consistent when setting limits?

You might wonder how important it is to be consistent when setting limits. Should you stick with a rule to help your child learn what's expected of him? Does consistency teach your child that he can't always have his way? Will bending the rules harm him or cause you to lose control?

When you're consistent, you provide your child with a sense of what is and isn't acceptable behavior. And in some areas, such as vital safety rules, consistency is essential. Yet, if you tried to enforce every rule you set, you'd spend so much of your time saying, "Don't do that," and "I already said you can't have that." Virtually every parent makes exceptions to the rules, depending on circumstance and personality. Some parents are quite flexible; others generally inflexible. Yet all parents find themselves at some point saying, "No, not today," then changing that to "Maybe," and finally saying, "Okay." This is part of parenting.

When one father took his daughter to a convenience store, she asked, "Can I get soda?" But her father said, "I'm only going in this store for milk and eggs." His daughter repeated, "But I want a Sprite for me." And her father said back, "I'm not buying you a soda, but I'll give you a drink when we get home." Minutes later the father and daughter walked out of the store. The father held his bag of eggs and milk, and his daughter walked out with a Sprite—with a straw in it.

You may fear that when you give in, your child will expect the same response the next time a similar situation arises. But as long as you're generally firm about discipline, you can make exceptions and still stay in control. When you show some flexibility and let your child know that his desires are important, and that life is not too rigid, he'll learn that sometimes people get what they want, and sometimes they don't, and he'll learn what compromise feels like.

You probably find that time, place, and mood influence your decision to stick to a rule or give in. That's okay. Sometimes you feel tolerant, and other times you're impatient and tired. In public, you don't want to be embarrassed by your child's behavior, so you might give in. You may be especially likely to give in when you need to distract your child because you're working or you're on the phone.

One mother wouldn't generally let her son mix spices and water together in a bowl as he had done with great enjoyment at a friend's house. But he learned a way around this. Whenever his mother took a business call, he would start getting spices off the shelf, usually with his mother's reluctant help. She needed to keep him quiet when she was on the phone and gave in.

If you're concerned about consistency, consider your overall relationship with your child. If you generally give the message that he's loved and accepted, and that you have basic, firm expectations about how he should behave, you don't have to worry about incidental exceptions you make. Being reasonably consistent is good enough. After all, you can't enforce a set of rules at all times. Flexibility is an important part of life, and give and take is an important part of parenting.

Can too much praise backfire?

To many people, praise seems like a great tool to use with kids. Praise helps them feel good about themselves and motivates them to do what pleases their parents. Yet too much praise, even when delivered with the best of intentions, can have a negative impact.

Your child has strong inner drives to accomplish things for herself and to succeed at many tasks. She's excited about learning, motivated to try new things, and eager to imitate adults. You can tell how proud your child is when she says, "Look, I got my shirt on by myself," or "I know how to count to ten." Her reward for these achievements is her own sense of accomplishment.

When you offer moderate praise for these achievements and reflect your child's own excitement ("I can see how happy you are"), she'll know that you're pleased. But when you give excessive praise ("Great job!" "I'm so proud of you!"), especially for everyday aspects of life such as toilet use or eating, or for a drawing she did or a puzzle she put together, your child may begin to expect such praise for everything she does. Eventually she may try to achieve not for internal satisfaction, but for the reward of praise, and her feelings of accomplishment may become of secondary importance. She may think, "I'll tie my shoe because Mom will think it's great."

Encouragement often works best, especially as a confidence booster: "You worked hard at building that tower, and you did it."

A child who's praised for every achievement may begin to distrust the praise and her own abilities. Is everything she does really that good? Or is anything she does really good at all? She may become dependent on praise and may not believe she's done something worthwhile unless she hears lavish compliments. Excessive praise can put pressure on her, too. When she's praised so heavily for doing well, she may feel she has to continue achieving or she'll lose the praise and attention. Many parents will understand these negative effects if they consider how dependent they, as adults, are on external praise and rewards.

It's fine to praise your child, and you certainly want to let her know that you feel good about her. But give praise in moderation and try to encourage her to feel good about her own abilities. Focus on her desire to do things for herself, and praise her by speaking more about her feelings than your own. "You really felt good about climbing that jungle gym, didn't you?" By responding that way, you recognize her pride in her success. You also can praise her effectively in nonverbal ways. A hug, a smile, and a look of approval all communicate your good feelings about her.

Is it okay to bribe children?

"If you ... then you can ..." It's a familiar pattern heard when parents try to persuade their child to do something. "If you come with me now, we'll stop at the park." "If you put your toys away, you can stay up fifteen minutes later." "As soon as you get in your car seat, I'll give you a treat."

There are always family struggles about the routines and necessities of life: bedtime, bathtime, shopping, leaving a friend's house, getting dressed, getting ready for school or day care. When logic fails (as it will), and your child refuses to do what you wish, you probably resort to bribing.

In theory, most parents are opposed to bribes. They want their children to cooperate and learn to tolerate frustration, and they don't want their children to expect rewards for good behavior. But it takes years for a child to learn self-control and to understand that certain things have to be done, even when people don't want to do them. Until a child can reason and motivate himself to do necessary tasks, bribery has its uses, and parents find that a bribe is a strong motivator.

One mother couldn't get her son to leave his friend's house, even though it was time for dinner. Finally she said, "If you come home now, you can paint with watercolors after dinner." After hearing this, her son agreed to leave. Another mother wanted to have her child come and play indoors, but he resisted. However, when she said, "Let's go in, and I'll play a game with you, and then we'll have a cookie," he came in. Incentives (which are the same as bribes, but sound and feel better to parents) such as these can distract or redirect a child and often eliminate struggles.

Bribes also can be used to avoid embarrassment. When you're out in public, you might offer a bribe rather than face a tantrum. That's okay. When you go shopping with your child, you may give him a cookie or toy to gain his cooperation and make the shopping trip go smoothly. This is also okay.

You may be worried that, once you offer a bribe in a situation, your child will expect one whenever a similar situation comes up. But this is rarely a problem, since children can accept compromise and a degree of inconsistency. If you bribed your child to go grocery shopping with you last week, but don't want to offer a bribe this week, let him know: "Last time I bought you gum, but today I'm not buying a treat." If necessary, distract him: "I like to bring you to the store so you can help pick out food for dinner." If you're firm and allow occasional rewards and compromises, he'll usually cooperate.

Sometimes, a way to eliminate the need for frequent bribes is to give your child plenty of warning when you want him to switch activities or go along with you cooperatively. If he's engrossed in play, tell him, "We need to go to the post office this afternoon." Then remind him ten minutes before you're ready to leave so he can bring his play to a pleasant, slow close. You can also let him know that he can leave his toys out so he can continue playing when he gets home. That way, he won't have to abruptly stop what he's doing or put his toys away in order to do what you want. And the chances are good that he'll come along peacefully, without needing a bribe.

Why does my child make such a mess?

Trying to clean up after young children is an endless task. They pull toys out of closets, drawers, and shelves, and when they're done playing with one thing, they drop it on the floor and get out something new. They also leave their clothes and shoes lying around. In just a short time, a young child can create a mess.

Some of this can be explained. Young children's interests shift quickly from one object to another, so even a brief play period may result in a big pile of toys. And because they like to play wherever their parents are, they carry (and leave) toys all over the house.

Most parents and young children argue over cleanup because parents care about keeping things neat and kids don't. Young children don't mind waking up, going to sleep, playing, and having friends over amid a jumble of toys. They aren't embarrassed for others to see a messy house and they don't understand when their parents get upset about their house not being in order.

You won't have success trying to get your child to think as you do about this issue, although you may be able to persuade or force your child to cleanup, using a variety of strategies, including punishments, consequences, or bribing: "If you put your toys away, you can have a playdate." Many children are reminded or punished over and over and still don't clean up after themselves. Their interests and energy are simply directed elsewhere.

The job of cleaning up usually is left for parents, and the daily process of putting things away can be both demanding and unrewarding. You may want or expect help from your child, but until children reach early elementary age, you'll get little relief. That's because your child doesn't think about cleaning up in the same way you do. Children are truly unaware of the tasks they leave for their parents.

Should I make my child clean up?

All parents must decide whether to constantly clean up after their children or let the cleaning go at times so the family can accomplish other things. Of course some adults care more about neatness than others. And some parents fear letting things get too messy because of unexpected visitors or the prospect of large-scale cleanups. Parents who work outside the home may feel a particular desire for a neat house because their cleanup time is so limited.

Although everyone would like help in maintaining a clean home, if you pressure your child to clean up, you may actually stifle her exploration and play—both a necessary part of childhood. For example, a child who's always expected to put her blocks away eventually may lose interest in using the blocks or may decide it's easier to simply watch TV. Also, those parents who feel compelled to establish early patterns of cleaning up may find the process frustrating and time-consuming. They usually have to stand over their young children and coach them through the entire chore. The effort expended in such supervising is often greater than the effort of cleaning up without the help. Many parents end up yelling day after day, "Put your toys away!"

Although cleaning up after young children remains an adult task, there are ways you can involve your child. Your two-and-a-half- or three-year-old can put a few toys back in place, particularly if you do the job with her or if you hand her the toys and tell her where they go. Your four- or five-year-old can take a more active role in straightening up, although she'll still be most successful when you're close by helping.

Your child may be willing to cooperate in cleanups if you give her some warning: "In five minutes it'll be time to put your toys away." If your child seems overwhelmed, help her focus by giving specific instructions: "Jesse, you're in charge of putting the puzzles and books away." Sometimes she'll go along with you if you offer concrete choices: "You can either put the trucks back on the shelf or put the toy soldiers in this basket." And when several children are playing together you can ask, "Who's going to put the crayons away? Who will clean up the train set?"

If your child resists putting her toys away, there are many other household jobs she may actually enjoy doing. These include dusting, washing windows, vacuuming, putting utensils away, or polishing silver. Children like to do what they watch their parents do, and they usually don't resist trying a new task.

The most successful and realistic way to handle cleaning up is to compromise and lower your standards. Straightening up is overwhelming to children. Don't punish or use harsh words with your child. Use a calm tone and offer to help: "I'll put the books back on the shelf while you put the doll clothes in the basket." Make cleanup playful: "Let's see how fast we can pick up these cards."

Don't worry about being consistent. Some days you'll care a lot about how your home looks, and other days you won't. You might even decide to ignore the mess unless company is expected. That's okay. Cleanup is a common problem and one that (in the grand scheme of raising children) is not worth battling over.

Chapter 5

THE PRESCHOOL YEARS: PLAYING NICE

- Why doesn't my child want to share?
- How can I teach my child to share her toys?
- Why isn't my child more considerate?
- What should I do when my child argues with her friends?
- Why isn't my child more reasonable?
- Why is my child uncomfortable kissing relatives?
- Is it all right for my child to call me by my first name?
- How can I teach my child to respect others?
- Should I ask my child to say "please" and "thank you"?
- How can I encourage my child to use polite words?
- Should I always make my child say, "I'm sorry"?
- Why do young children use bathroom language?
- How should I respond if my child uses profanity?
- What's the best way to introduce a new baby to an older sibling?
- How can I help my children get along with each other?
- How can I teach my child to be gentle with his pet?

Why doesn't my child want to share?

"It's mine!" screams a young boy, yanking a toy from another child.

"That's not nice," his mother says. "Michelle is your friend, and I want you to share with her."

"No, I want it!"

At times almost all young children have trouble sharing. While eighteen-month-olds grab toys from each other, conflicts over sharing peak between the ages of two and two and a half. Episodes of screaming, crying, and grabbing are not uncommon when children struggle for a toy.

Because a young child's thinking is egocentric, he sees things only from his own point of view and is unmoved by his parents' logical reasons for sharing. "Your friend wants to use this toy. How would you feel if he didn't share with you?" The question doesn't make sense to children, and it won't change their behavior. A child also won't be moved by his friend's obvious distress at not having a chance to share a toy. One three-and-a-half-year-old child became interested in her toy vacuum cleaner only after her friend took it out of the closet to use. A struggle ensued between the two children until the mother intervened. "Jesse was using the toy first. How would you feel if your friend Niki took her toys away from you while you were visiting her?" The child stood quietly with a blank look on her face and said, "It's my vacuum cleaner!" Such lack of concern for another's feelings may be difficult for parents to accept because adult thinking is so different from a young child's.

Parents who are frustrated or embarrassed by their child's unwillingness to share may blame themselves or have negative feelings about their child, considering him to be selfish or behaving inappropriately.

But once you realize that trouble with sharing is a normal aspect of development, you'll feel more comfortable and tolerant. Talking to other parents about sharing may also help. It's helpful to remember that sometimes even adults have problems sharing. People argue over parking spaces and cut each other off during rush hour. And an adult need only imagine a visiting friend opening drawers and looking at personal belongings to understand how a child feels about sharing his things.

How can I teach my child to share her toys?

Understanding your child's difficulty with sharing may bring some comfort, although you'll still have to deal with struggles over toys. Unfortunately, there are no magic answers to the problems of sharing, but there are things you can do to try to lessen the tension. First, you can try preparing your child (although this may not work). If a friend is coming to visit, say, "When Michelle comes over she'll want to play with your blocks, your puzzles, and the sliding board." Ask Michelle's parents to send along a little bag of toys for your child to play with. Your child will be easily distracted playing with toys that aren't his.

If your child grabs things from his friend, tell him, "Michelle's using that now, and when she's finished, you can use it." Sometimes you may want to set time limits for taking turns, but understand that your child may be frustrated by having to give up a toy he's playing with or trying to master. This is what time limits can feel like to a child: Imagine you're making a cake. You take out the ingredients, start to mix them, and then hear, "Time's up! It's Sharon's turn." You'd indignantly say, "I'm not done yet!" and even a few minutes more wouldn't help. That's how a child feels when forced to stop what he's doing and take turns.

When the struggle over toys becomes intense, you can try to interest your child in playing with something else. Or it may help to offer him choices: "Which toy would you like your friend to use—the ball or the puzzle?" You may have to distract your child by playing with him yourself or reading him a book. Although this can be frustrating, especially if you're involved in conversation with another adult, you should recognize that sharing conflicts among young children, and the resulting interruptions, are unavoidable.

Parents often find that sharing is easier if children play outside, if they play at a friend's house rather than at their own house, or if they're involved in something together, such as coloring, using play dough, or painting. Whatever you try, though, sharing will probably still be a problem. So have realistic expectations, understand sharing issues as a developmental phase, don't put too much pressure on your child, offer distractions, and set limits on the struggles. Also, remember to model the behavior you want your child to adopt. If you're giving and if you share courteously, your child will eventually copy you. Children learn more from parents' examples than from parents' admonitions.

Why isn't my child more considerate?

A four-year-old interrupted his mother's phone call: "Can I go outside?" She motioned for him to wait a minute, but he persisted. "Mom, Josh is outside. Can I play on his swings?" When she whispered for him to be quiet until she was off the phone, he walked away, but was back almost immediately. "Now can I go?" After hanging up, she felt frustrated with the interruptions and wondered why her son couldn't be more considerate and patient.

Children under the age of five or six have a difficult time thinking of other people's feelings. Young children, as researcher Jean Piaget pointed out, are egocentric; they focus on their own immediate needs and interests, and consider only one side of any situation—their own. They don't do this to be selfish, although that's often the result. They're generally incapable, during their early years, of putting themselves in another person's place or imagining how other people think and feel. Egocentrism is a normal, although difficult, part of child development.

Parents see egocentric thinking and behavior when children play. One child will grab another's toy, others will exclude some children from their play, and some call each other names. Young children don't think about how their words and actions impact others. They say, "You're not my friend anymore," or "You can't play with us," and often add, "You're not coming to my birthday party." When young children play board games, they often don't play by the rules or think about their opponent's chances. A child who drew an unfavorable card while playing a game said, "I'm just not listening to this card."

Parents try to change their children's actions and teach their children to stick to rules: "Don't hit; you'll hurt him," "He was using that," or "You should include her in your game." While these are good strategies, it's important to remember that young children have limited control over their thinking and often forget to (or just can't) consider others.

Frequent struggles over your child's self-centered ways can be very frustrating. You may wonder if your child is particularly unpleasant or if he acts selfish to "get at" you, and you may also wonder if you've set firm enough limits. You probably ask yourself, "Do other kids act this way?" When, for instance, your child doesn't let you rest ("Mom, look at my picture!") even when you're not feeling well, you may wonder if your child has any considerate feelings at all.

Although at times your child may act egocentric because you haven't set sufficient limits, more often he'll behave this way because he's just not yet able to consider other people's needs. Your expectations for his behavior should take into account this stage of development.

It's very important that you establish limits for your child, be a good role model for showing consideration, and teach him appropriate behavior. But you should also try to be flexible and patient as he grows through this stage and gradually learns to think about others' feelings and points of view. Of course, it's unrealistic to think you can always be understanding. You may often become angry at your child's thoughtless behavior, but understanding that this is a part of normal development is helpful. One mother became upset and embarrassed as she heard her daughter tell a boy who couldn't come to her birthday party, "Oh, goody. Now we'll have enough chairs." Expect to hear such statements, but also be assured that gradually, as your child matures, he'll learn to be more considerate of others' feelings.

What should I do when my child argues with her friends?

"Katie, let's play house. I'm the mommy; you're the baby."

"No, I'm the mommy, or I won't be your friend."

"Then I'm not playing with you."

This exchange is typical of what preschoolers say when they argue. They may play well together and then suddenly tell each other, "I'm not your friend." Young children, whose emotions are close to the surface, concentrate on their immediate wishes and needs. And because they're egocentric, they don't consider each other's feelings, but let their anger come out in harsh words or actions. Some children give in when spoken to in this way, while others fight back or persist until they get their way, or try to find an adult to help.

You may wonder what to do when you see this kind of behavior. You should begin by setting limits on your child, who is egocentric and needs your guidance; on her own, she doesn't think about others when she's mad. However, if you restrict her expressions of anger too much, she may end up believing that anger is bad and inappropriate.

Your child needs a chance to let her anger out, and even if you don't like to hear her say, "I'm not playing with you," or "You're not my friend anymore," you should realize that young children are not very good at expressing their exact thoughts. Harsh words are sometimes a young child's way of letting her strongest negative feelings be known. One five-year-old told her aunt, "You say 'nanny nanny boo boo' when someone takes your toy, and you get it back." She insisted, "You have to say that!"

When it seems appropriate, you can let arguing children try to work out their differences themselves, as long as no one is getting physically injured or having his or her feelings terribly hurt. Children are sometimes surprisingly good at settling their arguments and can gradually learn to work problems out with one another. A child who seldom has a chance to settle her own arguments may become dependent on her parents for help even with minor difficulties.

Parents should also step in and give suggestions and guidance. "Why don't you both pretend you're mommies and let your dolls be the babies?" If one child shouts something mean to another, parents should avoid saying, "That's not nice!" and instead say, "You're really mad because Tanya doesn't want you to play. Why don't you tell her that?" Even if angry children ignore parents' suggestions, the very presence of adults will have a restraining effect. Children tend to be less aggressive with each other when parents are nearby.

Young children also respond well when parents are clear. "You have to include her in your play." "He doesn't want you to yell at him, so you'll have to stop." "Tell her nicely what you want to do." "I know you're angry, but I won't let you be mean to her." And they benefit from their parent's support: "Let's go ask Sam if you can build the tower with him."

You can lessen your child's involvement in arguments by avoiding situations that usually lead to problems. For instance, your child may play well with one child at a time, but not when a third joins in. Three can be a difficult number—two friends sometimes pair up and exclude the third. If you can't avoid this situation, give all the children frequent reminders about getting along and including each other in play. If your child consistently argues with one particular playmate, limit their time together or tell them, "You have to find a way to get along with each other." Allow your child's emotions to be heard, but when necessary, help her control her anger by changing the situation or setting firm limits.

Why isn't my child more reasonable?

A father handed his daughter and her friend equal numbers of raisins. The daughter looked at the raisins on her and her friend's napkin and said, "Alison has more."

"But I gave you each the same amount," her father protested.

The girl refused to accept the facts and continued to argue, "Look, she has more."

Struggles often develop over such issues for children less than four or five years old. This is because young children base their reasoning on how things look, not necessarily on how things really are. One child wanted a whole cup of juice, but her mother only had half a cup left. The child fussed and refused the drink until her mother poured it into a tiny cup. The small amount of juice filled the little cup, and the child was happy, even though she still had the same amount of juice she had just refused as inadequate.

Parents can get easily frustrated when their child doesn't think logically. A parent can count out jellybeans to prove that all the children at a party have the same number, but the children often will not believe the shares are equal unless they "look" equal. A spread out pile may seem bigger than a compact one; a tall glass of juice may appear to hold more than a short, wide one. You can observe this pre-logical thinking with a simple experiment. Line up pennies in two identical rows (ten in each row), and ask your four- or five-year old child if both rows have the same number of pennies. Then let her watch as you spread one of the rows out. Then ask if both rows still have the same number of pennies. A child under five (or six) will say that the wider row now has more pennies in it, even though she saw that no new pennies were added. A child reasons, if it looks like more, it is more.

It's difficult, if not impossible, to change a young child's reasoning before she's developmentally ready to think logically. Once you realize that your child thinks differently than you do, you can understand why she so often rejects what seems perfectly reasonable. Between the ages of five and seven, you'll see dramatic changes in her thinking and reasoning abilities. Until then, try to accommodate her thinking and kid-like reasoning, rather than struggle to change her mind. A father whose child wanted more ketchup on her plate, even though she clearly had an adequate amount, simply spread the ketchup out so it looked like a larger amount. He avoided an argument, and his daughter was completely satisfied.

Why is my child uncomfortable kissing relatives?

In most families, children are expected to kiss their relatives hello and goodbye. When a child does this spontaneously, parents are pleased, and when he doesn't, they prompt him, "Give Grandma and Grandpa a kiss. They haven't seen you in such a long time." Parents often feel that they'll be judged unfavorably if their child doesn't give a kiss.

Yet many children are uncomfortable kissing their relatives and often don't want to do it. This can create an awkward situation, especially when a relative feels rejected by the child or feels that he's not excited to see her. And if the relative has brought him a gift and still doesn't get a kiss, she might feel particularly frustrated and begin to say negative things. "What's the matter with him? Is he shy?" The uneasy parent might urge him to "give Aunt Sue a kiss since she gave you a present." This can put a great deal of pressure on the child, who will usually give in if harassed enough. But the resulting discomfort for the child and his parents is often not worth the struggle.

A child who resists giving a kiss is probably not rejecting a relative. Most children are excited about seeing family members, but feel uneasy giving a kiss hello for any of a number of reasons. A child may not be comfortable with the physical contact of a kiss or, feeling shy and self-conscious, may reject kissing because he doesn't like to be focused on. He may be busy playing or want to stay close to his parents, even cling to them, until he feels adjusted to the visitors or to being in a relative's house.

Sometimes a relative is one the child rarely sees, and he resists kissing because he needs time to get used to a strange face. A few children have private or magical concerns about kissing. One five-year-old worried that he would "turn old" if he kissed his aunt, while another child reported that she didn't want to kiss her relatives because "people give you germs on your lips." And at times a child won't give a kiss goodbye because he doesn't want a visit to end, although he's too young to explain this.

If you're faced with a resisting child, try to let the kiss go—most children just need time to ease into a visit and feel friendly. Instead of insisting, suggest other options for your child. He could tell his relatives about something that has recently happened, demonstrate a new skill, or show them a favorite possession. And even if he won't kiss, he may willingly "give five," shake hands, blow a kiss, or give a hug good-bye.

We can all remember being small and feeling the pressure to give a kiss or having a relative demand a kiss. If we recall how we felt then, we can understand our own children's reluctance to give kisses and can help them find other ways to begin and end visits with relatives.

Is it all right for my child to call me by my first name?

It's very common for a first-born child between the ages of eighteen months and three years to call her parents by their first names. She imitates what she hears, and since her parents and their friends, neighbors, and relatives all use first names when talking to each other, she uses first names too.

Many parents don't mind if their young child occasionally uses first names, although some consider anything other than "Mommy" and "Daddy" disrespectful. When your child uses your first names, she intends no disrespect—usually she's just mimicking what other people say. Over time, this imitative behavior will diminish, and your child will stop using your first names.

If you're bothered or embarrassed when your child calls you by your first name, remind her to say "Mommy" and "Daddy." But remember that it'll be hard for her, especially if she's under two, to call you "Mommy" and "Daddy" consistently, since she doesn't usually hear other people call you that. If you have a second child, you'll notice that he or she rarely uses your first name. That's because there's an older sibling to copy and because the second child is used to hearing "Mommy" and "Daddy."

A common question related to first-name use is, "What should my child's friends call me?" Some parents are most comfortable with first names and believe they're easier for young children to remember and use. Other parents want to be called "Mrs.," "Ms.," or "Mr." Whichever makes you and others comfortable, your child will follow your lead.

How can I teach my child to respect others?

There are two ways your child learns about respect. He listens to what you say about respectful behavior, and he copies the way you usually act. Ultimately, your child will learn more from your actions than from your words. If you treat your child and others courteously, he'll eventually copy your behavior. But if you speak harshly to him—"Get over here now!"—and consistently belittle him when he expresses his needs or makes mistakes, he will not learn to treat others with respect, even if you admonish him to behave well.

Day care and nursery-school teachers sometimes say they can tell how respectful parents are by listening to their children playing. When two preschoolers pretend they have a crying baby, one might say, "Let's pick her up. She's crying," while the other might reply, "You get out of this house right now, and take this crying baby with you."

A young child doesn't automatically know how to act appropriately. He has to have good models, and be taught and frequently reminded, since he's egocentric and easily forgets about other people's feelings when his own needs are strong. Parents often feel defeated after telling their child again and again to be nice to others, only to see him act selfishly again. At such times, it's important to remember that learning to show respect is a slow process, and that it's natural for young children to think mainly of themselves.

If you feel constantly unhappy with your child's disrespectful behavior, perhaps you should reevaluate your expectations. It's possible that you're asking for more than he's capable of. The younger he is, the less likely he is to control his emotions and put himself in someone else's place. Therefore, it's necessary for you to put limits on his behavior: "You can't say mean words to your sister."

Look for ways you can model respectful behavior: "Let me pick you up so you can see better," or "Let's go over there and thank that man for helping us." Consistently use a respectful tone and respectful words with your child. When children are respected, they internalize feelings of self-worth, believing that their ideas, needs, and desires are important. Over time, your child will give back the kind of respect you've given him, and you'll see him begin to consider other people's needs and feelings.

Should I ask my child to say "please" and "thank you"?

"Mia, how do you ask for something?" "Now what do you say to Uncle Marty?" "What's the magic word?" A child who's questioned like this may mumble a faint "please" or "thank you," and parents may feel somewhat reassured. But they may also wonder why they have to constantly remind their child to use polite words.

When children say "please" and "thank you" without being prompted or coerced, parents feel a sense of satisfaction. They're proud when their child is polite in public, and they feel good when she's polite at home. Children make so many requests throughout the day: "I want juice!" "I need a napkin!" "Tie my shoe!" Toddlers point to what they want or use one word to describe what they want, "Cookie!" When a child says "please" and remembers to say "thank you," parents often feel good and less overwhelmed, and have an easier time responding to her constant needs.

So why don't most young children say "please" and "thank you" spontaneously? And why do many parents find themselves in situations such as this: A mother preparing to leave a neighborhood party tells her three-year-old daughter, "Say 'good-bye' and 'thank you' to Mrs. Miller." Her child turns away and refuses to speak, as other mothers stare at her. She tries again, then thanks the hostess herself and leaves, feeling embarrassed by her child's impoliteness.

Yet when children forget or refuse to say "please" and "thank you," they're usually not being impolite. There are several explanations for their behavior. First, they have a difficult time grasping general rules, including ones about responding in socially appropriate ways. A child who's told to say "thank you" when given something at Grandma's house may not connect that experience to a similar one that happens later at a neighbor's house. Although she's again being given something, she's too young to understand that she should respond as she did earlier.

Another reason children may not use polite words is shyness. While some children respond to prompting, others are just too self-conscious, especially when adult attention is focused on them. A shy child may refuse to say "please" or "thank you," and this can lead to a struggle if parents force the issue.

Finally, a child may be too preoccupied to say "please" and "thank you," especially if she's just been given a new toy or has an urgent request. She has a difficult time thinking about and considering other people's wishes, and saying what her parents want her to say may be the furthest thing from her mind when she's excited.

If you constantly remind your child to say "please," you might put yourself in a bind. You may inadvertently convince her that her wishes will be granted if she uses what, for her, may actually seem like a magic word. For example, in a toy store she may say, "Please, Mom, please. Will you buy this for me?" When you explain why she can't have the toy she just politely asked for, she may not understand (or not want to hear) your reasoning. "But I said please!" Since you want to encourage politeness, you may be reluctant to say "no." Inevitably, your child will receive a confusing mixed message—saying "please" sometimes gets her what she asks for and sometimes doesn't.

How can I encourage my child to use polite words?

If your child doesn't often say "please" and "thank you" on her own, there are a number of things you can try. Watch for times when she uses polite words, and reinforce that behavior by saying, "I really like the way you asked for that." If you know that your child is too shy to say "thank you," you can do the thanking for her, which may make you both more comfortable and let you model polite behavior for her. And if you're unhappy with the way she's asked for something, say, "When you ask me that way, it doesn't make me want to give you juice," or "You'll have to find another way of asking." Such statements give her an opportunity to say "please" or to change her tone of voice.

Tone is very important. As adults, we're usually more concerned about using a polite tone than about always attaching "please" to our requests. When your child makes frequent demands ("Zip my jacket!"), you may be so frustrated with her tone that you find yourself harshly demanding politeness ("PLEASE!"). If she mimics that harsh "please," you still won't like the way she sounds. But, if instead of demanding a "please," you model the right tone, she may understand what you want, and she'll learn to respond more pleasantly.

Finally, and most importantly, remember to say "please" and "thank you" when you ask your child for something or when she's done what you've requested. And remember to speak politely to others. All too often we make demands of children and others without ever saying "please" and "thank you" to them. When your child hears you speaking politely to her and to other children and adults, she'll begin to do as you do.

Should I always make my child say, "I'm sorry"?

A mother sees her son hit his friend and says, "That wasn't nice. Now tell him you're sorry." Her son reluctantly mutters, "Sorry," but it's clear he feels no remorse. In fact, he probably believes he did nothing wrong. Young children are egocentric and often focus on fulfilling their own needs without considering other people's feelings. At times, they grab, hit, knock over each other's blocks, say unkind things, and refuse to share. When these things happen, you should set firm limits rather than coerce your child into making insincere apologies.

When a child is forced to apologize, and when saying "I'm sorry" is the main consequence for unacceptable behavior, he may decide that it's worth hitting other children or knocking over their toys. All he has to do is apologize afterwards, and he may be excused without further consequences.

Parents often enforce an apology because it's a quick and easy way to deal with misbehavior. Yet parents know that hearing their child say, "I'm sorry," can at times be unsatisfying. When they talk to their child about his unacceptable actions, he may respond, "But I said I'm sorry." If you don't overemphasize apologies, your child can't so easily "get off the hook."

The real motivation for a child to change his behavior comes not from the fear of having to apologize, but from the fear of angering his parents, or having a toy or privilege taken from him. A child who doesn't want his parents to get angry at him may apologize on his own for misbehavior. Such an apology comes from within him and is much more sincere than an apology he's forced to make.

You may wonder why your child doesn't make genuine apologies. Sometimes he's too embarrassed or ashamed to admit wrongdoing, and at other times he may not like being put on the spot. He may deny his actions ("I didn't do it!") either because he actually believes it's true or because he fears your reaction and disapproval. Often, young children have strong feelings of autonomy and resist doing what their parents want them to do.

When your child hurts another child, focus on setting limits. Rather than saying, "You hit her; now apologize," say, "I'm not going to let you hit her," or "You may not want to play with your brother, but I'm not going to let you hurt him." If you think your child's old enough to understand, you can have him help remedy a situation: "Since you pushed over your friend's blocks, you'll have to help her put her building back together." You can also model considerate behavior by apologizing for him: "I'm sorry he pushed over your building. He's going to help you build it again."

The older your child gets, the more easily you can discuss angry feelings with him. Listen to his reasons for misbehavior, no matter how far-fetched they seem: "But I had it first," "He hit me," or "He wouldn't let me play." Before he can learn to offer sincere apologies, he needs to believe that he can explain his side of a disagreement. Children (and adults) who feel unheard often defend themselves and, unless coerced, refuse to apologize even when they know they're wrong.

Since your child imitates your behavior, remember to apologize to him when you overreact, bump into him, or take him away from play to rush out for your own reasons. If you apologize whenever the situation calls for it, your child will eventually copy your words and actions.

Why do young children use bathroom language?

"Mason, what are you going to be for Halloween?"

"Doo doo face," says Mason, and both children laugh.

Young children think it's funny to say such words as "doody," "pee pee," "boobies," and "butt." The words are not quite "bad," but to children they have their power. They use bathroom language when they feel silly or need a quick way to be funny and make their friends laugh. The words also provide a way of releasing tension and getting attention. A child might use bathroom words more than usual when there's a new baby in her family, when she's unhappy in day care or school, or when she wants the attention of a friend who's playing with someone else. Using these words often does bring a child instant attention from adults and friends.

Different parents have different reactions to bathroom language. Some just shrug their shoulders and ignore the words. Others are annoyed or embarrassed and wonder where their child learned such language. They worry that she'll be reprimanded by a teacher or caregiver, and wonder if her use of bathroom language is a reflection of their parenting.

You should feel reassured to know that all children use bathroom words, which they hear and repeat at school and at home. It's almost impossible to delete the words from your child's vocabulary. Of course, it's not as upsetting when a three-year-old uses bathroom language as it is when a five-year-old uses these words. The best you can do is ignore it or set limits. "I don't want you to talk that way," or simply, "We don't use those words in our house." If you think your child's using bathroom language for attention, she probably needs more time with you. Play with her more, read to her more, and spend more time nurturing her interests. But don't dwell on the fact that she's using bathroom language. This is just normal preschool silliness.

How should I respond if my child uses profanity?

Parents often forget that children are active listeners and imitators. If parents use profanity (and most do, either regularly or during moments of anger), so will their children. And children are surprisingly good mimics. They swear with their parents' tone and intensity, and they use curse words in the appropriate contexts. Young children pick up profanity, which they also hear from playmates and on TV, just as they pick up other phrases. When one four-year-old heard a loud noise in his house, his parents were surprised to hear him ask, "What the h— was that?"

If you respond with surprise when your child uses a curse word, or when you say, "Don't ever use that word again," your child will learn that profanity has power: "Mom, Anton said a bad word!" Your child may continue to use swear words (or other words you disapprove of) to test out their shock value and to try to understand what makes certain words bad.

Parents are usually alarmed if they hear their child use profanity. They feel embarrassed, worry that he'll be blamed for teaching these words to other children, and wonder how to get their child to stop. Parents also worry that his cursing will reflect on the entire family and that people may assume such language is used and condoned in their home. Because of these fears, many parents become angry and react strongly when their child uses profanity. But parents should be careful not to blame their child for his natural tendency to imitate what he hears.

If your child uses swear words only occasionally, there's no need to be concerned. But if he uses such words often, there are several things you can do. The most important is to stop using profanity yourself. If he no longer hears the words from you (or from the TV shows you let him watch), he'll probably stop cursing. You can also set firm limits on his language, "That's not a nice word," or "We don't use that word in our house." Typically if you don't overreact, and continue to monitor your own language, your child will stop using profanity.

What's the best way to introduce a new baby to an older sibling?

Family dynamics change drastically when a second child is born. While parents give constant care to their infant, their older child often reacts negatively because of the major adjustments she has to make. Reactions vary, of course, with the age of the older sibling.

A four- or five-year-old will be much more independent and under-standing than a one- to three-year-old, but all older siblings will have some negative feelings. The way parents respond to their older child's feelings about the baby often sets the tone for the children's future relationship.

Some parents who pressure their older child to love the baby, try to censure their child's feelings: "Don't say that about your little brother—it's not nice." A child who's not allowed to share her nega-tive feelings with her parents will continue to have those feelings; she'll just express them in other ways. She may not take her anger out on her parents, since she, like all young children, fears losing their love, but she may take her anger out on her sibling.

Your older child needs the freedom to express her negative feel-ings so she can resolve them. Allow her to say, "Take the baby back to the hospital," and show that you understand her situation by saying, "It's sometimes hard, isn't it, to have a new baby in the house." She'll begin to accept and even like the baby once she knows that she can express her dislike without risking your love and accep-tance. The more she's accepted and reassured, the more likely she is to develop positive feelings about her sibling, although there will always be some negative emotions as well.

Your older child will begin to feel good about her sibling when the baby starts smiling, giggling, and seeking her out. "He likes me!" Support and encourage this early interaction by saying, "Yes, he really does like you. He thinks you're funny and nice." At this point, she might enjoy helping you take care of the baby.

How can I help my children get along with each other?

As your children grow, you'll have to consciously encourage them to respect each other. When they show consideration, give them positive feedback. "That was nice of you to pick up his toy." "Thanks for letting him play with you and your friend." If you treat each of your children with love, and show that you accept them and their similarities and differences, they'll respond positively.

Don't make one child seem more important or more deserving of consideration than the other. If you say, "Let him do it—he's younger," or "She's older, so she can go," or "She's better at it, so let her go first," you'll give your children reasons to feel resentful and jealous, and you'll encourage a cycle of competitiveness. And if you say, "The baby needs to be carried, but you're big enough to walk," or "Don't play with the baby's toys. You're too old for that," your older child will feel anger that will be directed at her younger sibling, not at you.

At times you may sympathize with your older child, but be careful not to encourage her negative feelings. Listen to her complaints about her younger sibling, but don't say, "Yes, he really is a nuisance, isn't he?" She'll consider your comments a license to feel and say what she wants about her sibling, and your younger child may end up feeling rejected.

Be matter-of-fact about the different things you do with your children. "She's going to bed later because she slept later this morning," or "I'm putting this together for him because he doesn't understand how to do it."

If your children are close in age and argue over toys, try to downplay the issue of possessions. Rather than say, "That's his toy," encourage them to share and trade their playthings, and provide some toys that will interest both. If your younger child wants to play with something that belongs to his sibling, distract the older one for a moment so the younger has a chance with the toy. Then thank your older child for sharing, even though she did not do so intentionally.

Allow them to work out some of their minor problems themselves, and try not to take sides. Too often parents end up blaming quarrels on the older child, "who should know better." When this happens, the older child gets angry at her parents for scolding her, but she takes out her anger on her sibling because he's a safer target.

Generally, set firm limits and send a consistent message about getting along in your family: "You need to find a way to use the toy together." "Let her play with you." "I won't let you exclude your brother." "Talk nicely to each other." Children can learn to follow your rules about getting along way before they understand the value of family harmony.

In spite of all you do to encourage a good relationship, your children will still argue with each other, probably every day. Try to understand and accept that some arguments are inevitable. And take comfort and pleasure in the times you see your children showing genuine love and consideration for each other.

How can I teach my child to be gentle with his pet?

It's not unusual for a young child to handle his pet a bit roughly. He may touch its eyes, pull its fur, put his fingers in its ears, and even sit on it. One child carried her hamster in a bag, while another let his pet gerbil "have fun rolling down the steps."

Parents frequently react to such mistreatment by saying, "How would you like it if someone did that to you?" One veterinarian became so irritated by the way his daughter carried the family's new dog that he carried his daughter around the same way to show her what such treatment felt like. However, logic and examples have little effect on children under five, who have a difficult time putting themselves in another person's (or pet's) place.

Your child doesn't mean to cause harm when he mishandles his pet. He just intends to play with it and explore it, and he doesn't understand the consequences of his actions. In fact, most children are very fond of their pets and develop strong emotional attachments to them. One child, seeking acceptance after his father disciplined him, hugged his cat and said, "You like me; you're my friend." Children often share feelings with their pets. "Mommy won't let me go outside and I want to."

Your child may feel a great deal of affection for his pet, but if he's under five years old, you've probably seen him mistreat the animal. In order to protect your pet, show your child exactly how to handle it, and be prepared to remind him of this often. You may also have to set consequences: "If you handle the dog roughly, you won't be allowed to play with him."

If your child is four or five years old, consistent reminders ("Touch Chloe softly") and firm limits ("That's too rough") should work, but if he's three or under, he's too young to remember how to play with a pet safely. In any case, you'll need to supervise closely when your child plays with his pet. Because watching a young child and a pet takes a lot of time and energy, many parents decide not to get a pet until their child is at least five years old. At this age, a child has an easier time understanding how a pet should be handled.

Chapter 6

IMAGINATION, CREATIVITY, AND PLAY

- Why does my child have an imaginary friend?
- How should I react to my child's imaginary friend?
- What does my child think about nature?
- My child asks questions and talks all the time. Is this normal?
- Does my child know what's real and what's not?
- What toys will my four- and five-year-old like?
- What are some good homemade toys?
- Do coloring books limit creativity?
- Why does my child always say, "Watch me, Mom!"?
- Should my child play with children his own age?
- How can I encourage art at home?
- How should I react to my child's artwork?

Why does my child have an imaginary friend?

Many parents worry when their child, usually between the ages of three and five, creates an imaginary friend. "Why does he need one? Can't he tell the difference between a real person and a pretend one?" And while they're sometimes amused by their child's concerns ("Watch out! You'll sit on Herman!"), they're more often frustrated.

Yet an imaginary friend is an important and creative part of growing up for many children. The friend helps a child deal with emotions and problems that he might otherwise not be able to handle. For example, a child might invent a companion as a way of relieving loneliness when he moves to a new home, leaving his real friends behind. Or the imaginary friend might help him deal with a new baby in the family, the start of day care or nursery school, or tension at home. Sometimes a child creates an imaginary animal, such as a dog, to help overcome a fear of real dogs or because he wishes to have a dog.

If a child feels overly controlled or unaccepted by his parents, he may invent a companion who's very accepting and who always likes him. He may even become a demanding "parent" to his friend, whom he imagines to be a powerless child. "Herman, that was very bad. You shouldn't have done that."

Sometimes a child will use an imaginary friend to relieve himself of guilt. Since a child who's done something wrong often fears discipline, he may deny his misbehavior ("I didn't do it") even when he's been caught. If a child fears rejection, he may blame his imaginary friend for his own misdeeds. That way he will not have to deal with criticism or responsibility. "Herman took the papers off your desk," or "Herman made me do it."

How should I react to my child's imaginary friend?

If your child has an imaginary friend, you may wonder what to do about it. Should you set an extra place at the table, as your child requests, or will your acceptance of the companion just prolong the fantasy? Compromise is the best solution. It's certainly all right to go along with some of your child's requests for his imaginary friend. And as long as you're patient with your child, it's also all right to set limits: "You may talk about your friend, but we're not going to change our routine for him right now." If you're worried because your child believes in an imaginary character, keep in mind that we encourage children to believe in the tooth fairy, Santa Claus, and other pretend characters. The main difference between these and your child's friend is that the friend is your child's own creation.

If you think your child is involved in fantasy because he feels powerless, consider the amount of freedom you allow him. You may want to give him more opportunities to express his feelings, make decisions ("I don't want to eat that"), and explore. And if your child seems lonely because of a recent move or the lack of nearby playmates, help him to find real friends who can eventually take the place of the imaginary one.

As your child grows, he will give up his pretend companion, and in time, he and you will look back on this short phase as simply an interesting part of growing up.

What does my child think about nature?

A young child's thoughts about the world are not based on logic and fact. When a child under four or five is asked about the sun, he may explain that a man lit a match and threw it up in the sky, and that's how the sun got there. Young children often believe that humans created the oceans, trees, space, mountains, and other natural phenomena. A child will ask, "Why did they make that mountain so high? Why did they put Switzerland so far away?" After a snowstorm, one child said, "I guess the people ran out of snowflakes."

Young children assume that inanimate objects have the same motives, intentions, and feelings a child has. One boy looked in his bucket after a downpour and said, "Guess what the rain did. It gave me water. Wasn't that nice?" Another child, trying his bike for the first time in several months, declared, "Look, my bike got smaller!" Sometimes a child will blame an object for a mishap: "That chair bumped into me!" And when a child misses a ball during a game of catch, he may not feel badly about his own abilities: "That ball started flying crooked."

To a young child, many objects are alive—a pencil because it writes, a cloud because it moves. Picture books and fairy tales enchant him because they mirror his world by presenting talking objects and animals, and trees that walk and sing.

To find out what your child thinks about nature and the objects around him, listen to his explanations of events, and ask, "How do you think the stars got there? Why do you think worms crawl?" When he asks you a question, ask for his thoughts before you answer. You'll be delighted with his responses and fascinated by the insights you get into his thinking. Keep asking and noticing how his answers change as he grows older.

You may be tempted to correct your child when he gives you answers that are clearly not factual. Sometimes it's best to just accept what he says, although at other times you'll want to offer as much information as you think he can understand. But don't be surprised if he listens and then sticks to his own thoughts and beliefs. This is natural behavior for children under five or six years old, who generally stick to their own ideas about the world.

My child asks questions and talks all the time. Is this normal?

Young children are natural learners and great observers of the here and now. They constantly try to gather information about what goes on around them, and that means they ask many questions and talk a lot: "Who's that?" "Why is she doing that?" "Where is that truck going?" Since a child believes that adults know everything, she assumes that her parents will have the answer to each question. She also assumes that everything has a purpose that can be discovered just by asking: "Why is that man so tall?"

Sometimes a child uses questions to relieve her anxieties. She may ask, "Why is that dog barking?" because she's afraid of the dog. At other times, she might ask a stream of questions or talk on and on just to be sociable and stay in constant contact with her parents.

Many times, as soon as you've answered your child's question, she'll ask the same question again or follow your explanation with an immediate "Why?" This can be annoying because you may feel that you're constantly responding to your child. At times it's hard to know what your child wants, since she's often not satisfied by your explanations. If you question her before you offer a complex answer, you may gain some insight into her real needs: "What do you think that word means?" "Tell me why you think that man was running."

Sometimes your child will repeatedly ask "why" and reject an answer because she doesn't understand it. She may have difficulty absorbing facts that aren't familiar or that don't relate directly to her experience. That's why parents should answer questions on a level that's appropriate for their child. And they should expect to hear the same questions over and over because it takes time and repetition before a child can master complex information.

Your child may occasionally ask a question that's difficult to answer. One four-year-old from a family with three children asked her friend's mother, "Why do you only have two kids?" The mother, concerned that the child might be upset by an honest answer (two was all she wanted), put the question back to the child, "Why do you think I only have two children?" She replied, "Because you wanted to," and was satisfied.

A problem often arises when young children ask socially embarrassing questions. You may be in a store with your child when she points to someone and loudly asks, "Why is he so fat?" She has no understanding of the man's feelings and asks only because she's spontaneous and curious. Yet you'll naturally feel ashamed and sorry. The best you can do at such moments is give her a brief, quiet answer ("That's just the way he looks"), and then try to distract her or promise to discuss the situation later.

When your child's constant questions and general chatter bother you, remember that she's curious and interested in what goes on around her, and you're the one she'll ask to get answers to her questions. Let her know that you're interested and listening, even if at times you just acknowledge her talk by nodding or saying, "I'm listening," or even, "Um-hmm." Listening to her questions will help you gain insight into how your child thinks.

Does my child know what's real and what's not?

Young children often believe that whatever they hear and see is real. Until a child is between five and seven years old, his experience is limited, and his ability to reason is not fully developed; therefore he can't truly be logical. It may not make sense to an adult, but to a young child, clowns are real, everything on TV is true, everything other children say is true, and a disguise changes a person. A young child's inability to distinguish make-believe from reality explains his fear of monsters, masks, and costumed figures.

When a young child watches television, he thinks he's watching real life. One four-year-old saw a Superman program followed by a televised demonstration intended to prove that Superman really didn't fly. A man lay down on a table and showed how camera tricks simulate flying. After the demonstration, the child's mother asked if he still thought Superman could fly. "Yes," he answered, "but that man on the table can't."

It's very difficult to convince a child that television doesn't always represent the truth. Toys in commercials look magical and exciting as they talk and move around on their own. It takes years for a child to develop some skepticism about these advertisements. One young boy insisted that sugared cereal was good for him, because television had told him so. His mother explained the purpose of commercials, but he still believed what he'd heard.

Just as a child believes what he hears on television, he also believes what other people, including other young children, say. If his friend says, "There are bugs under your rug," or "The moon is a dead planet," or, in a moment of anger, "You're not coming to my party," a child may accept the statement as truth without questioning the other child's knowledge or motives.

Words are taken literally and have tremendous power. That's why a young child gets so upset when he's called "a dummy;" he feels he must shout back, "No, I'm not," or get someone else to reassure him. Children, especially those under three, usually can't separate names or descriptions from objects and people. A mother told her son that he was handsome, and he said, "No, I'm not. I'm Jimmy." It takes time for children to realize that names are not parts of things but are separate and often changeable.

Young children can be confused not just by what they hear and see, but by what they imagine and dream. They aren't sure what dreams are or where they come from: Do they come from the sky? The bed? The toys the child sleeps with? Through the window? Frightening dreams seem very real, and vivid dreams seem part of real life. One child, who had dreamed that an airplane landed in the park behind his house, woke up believing the plane was really there. When his father tried to convince him otherwise, he refused to listen. The father finally took his son to the park to show him that there was no plane.

You can find out what your child thinks by questioning him, listening to him, and observing him. You'll find that his thinking is different from that of adults and that he believes many things that aren't true. As long as your child bases his thinking on appearances and his own experience (which is part of normal development), you may not be able to change his mind on many issues, but as he nears elementary-school age, your child's logical understanding of the world will increase.

What toys will my four- and five-year-old like?

Play is an essential part of growing up. When your child plays freely, he satisfies his curiosity and finds out how to use objects; he learns to plan and classify; he begins to evaluate, predict, question, discover, draw conclusions, and solve problems; and he also learns how to interact with his peers and imitate the people around him. A child whose play is not controlled and channeled by adults ("The colors in that painting should really be blue and green." "If you pile any more blocks up, your building will fall.") gains confidence through play and rarely has a fear of failure.

Some parents minimize the importance of play, looking instead for "educational" or prepackaged activities for their child. But your child really doesn't need these in order to learn. You can nurture his drive to learn by following up on his interests, giving him many opportunities to play, and providing appropriate toys and materials.

A four- or five-year-old child will like using arts and crafts materials such as pens, pencils, markers, scissors, tape, glue, string, play dough, clay, watercolors, tempera (which can be mixed with soap flakes to help prevent stains), and finger paints. Wagons, Big

Wheels, scooters, and bikes with or without training wheels are fun, as are balls, bats, frisbees, bubble blowers, kites, bowling pins, balance boards, old tires to swing or jump on, and bean bags to toss. While games like Candy Land, Hungry Hungry Hippos, Sorry, and various matching games are popular, young children often don't play by the rules because they don't want to lose. If this is the case with your child, choose other activities he enjoys, and trust that as he gets older, he'll want to follow the rules.

You can also give your child practical things to play with, such as flashlights; magnifying glasses; whistles; simple tools; old household objects he can safely take apart; a bank and coins; child-size rakes and snow shovels; a funnel, pump, and eggbeater to use while playing with water and bubbles; and a large plastic needle with yarn for sewing burlap. Your child may enjoy building with Tinker Toys, Legos, and all kinds of blocks, and may want to make forts and houses out of blankets or large cardboard boxes. You can help your child make a puppet theater from a table turned on its side; he can run the show with play tickets, play money, and a toy cash register. A toy (or real) microphone is fun for kids who like to sing and dance. A child this age is influenced by his friends and by TV, and may want whatever toy other children have.

When you provide toys for a child of any age, avoid giving too many that limit creative play. So many toys can only be put together and used in one way, and if your child spends all his time with such toys, he'll have little chance to make his own creations. Instead look for toys that can be used in a variety of ways and ones that allow him to use his imagination. For example, instead of buying kits of shrinkable plastic with pre-drawn pictures, buy the same plastic, without the drawings, at a craft store. Then your child can make his own designs.

As you buy toys, you may find that your child becomes intensely interested in a new plaything for several weeks and then loses interest. This is common, although it may be disturbing if you've spent time and energy shopping for the right toy, one your child said he "wanted so badly." He loses interest for several reasons: he may have quickly exhausted all the toy's play possibilities, he may have mastered the toy, figuring out how it works, or he may be frustrated because it isn't made well or is difficult to use.

To get more use from your child's discarded but almost-new toys, put them away in a closet for several months. When you take them out, they'll seem unfamiliar to your child, and he may become interested in them again. He may even think of new ways to play with them, since his interests and his play are always changing.

They often play out real experiences or feelings. In pretend "school," a child can be the teacher and fantasize about having control. "You need to stop talking." "It's time to hear a story." When they play house, they take roles that make them feel comfortable. One might choose to be a decision-making parent, while another wants to be a baby who cries and needs nurturing. Superhero play lets children feel strong and powerful. Some parents object to imaginary violence; however, pretend fighting games are a normal part of play. If parents are watchful, such games won't get out of control.

Many kids get involved in big, dramatic projects—building a fort, designing a haunted house or a house out of blankets, putting on a puppet show, or creating a garden. They thrive on these activities and proudly show off the results.

If your child has an interest in such projects, offer him support. If, for example, he wants to build, help him find materials. He'll make good use of large boxes, scraps of wood, sheets, and blankets. Once he's carried out a large project, he'll feel successful and competent.

In one neighborhood, five-year-olds wanted to put on a play. Parents provided dress-up clothes and paper and paints, and the children spent time preparing and rehearsing. In another neighborhood, several kindergarten children and their parents used scraps of wood to build a playhouse. When the kids finished their project, they not only had a playhouse, but a strong sense of satisfaction and accomplishment.

What are some good homemade toys?

Although stores offer a multitude of toys, you can create kits and playthings that provide enjoyment and encourage your child to be creative. The following are suggestions for games, toys, and gifts for two- to five-year-olds. The kits take time to assemble, but probably no more time than searching stores for the "right" toy. And your child will have fun helping you put these playthings together and decorating storage boxes with crayons or contact paper. Choose materials that are appropriate for your child's age and supervise as he plays.

Art Box

In a plastic or cardboard shoe box, place any of the following supplies: colored pencils, magic markers, crayons, chalk, yarn, string, pipe cleaners, watercolor paints with brushes, small sheets of paper, a small canvas, glue, tape, tissue paper, felt, scraps of fabric, a ruler, old greeting cards, Popsicle sticks, strips of cardboard or balsa wood, scissors, and a hole puncher.

Play Office

In a large plastic or cardboard file box place any of the following: a calculator, a clipboard, a clock, an old cell phone, a toy computer, a loose-leaf binder with paper, stationery, a calendar, 3x5 index cards, Post-it notes, folders, pencils and pens, envelopes, paper clips, an eraser, stickers, stamps and a stamp pad, and rubber bands.

Tool Box

For three-year-olds and up, make a kit including basic tools, measuring tape, sandpaper, wood pieces, and Styrofoam pieces. Use toy tools for the youngest children. Older children can use real tools under your close supervision.

Play Dough

To make your own play dough, use the following ingredients: one cup of flour, one-half cup of salt, two teaspoons of cream of tartar, one cup of water, two tablespoons of oil, and one tablespoon of food coloring (optional). Combine the first three ingredients in a large saucepan. Gradually stir in the water mixed with the oil and food coloring. Cook over medium heat, stirring constantly until a ball forms. Remove the dough from the heat and knead it until it is smooth. The dough can be stored in plastic bags or containers, and put in a kit with a rolling pin, small cups, an empty egg carton, empty thread spools, plastic knives, or other objects that would be fun to use with play dough.

Sewing Kit

In a cardboard box or a lunch box, place cardboard, poster board, large plain file cards, a hole puncher, string, buttons, a plastic needlepoint needle, yarn, burlap, and scissors.

Forest Ranger or Camper Kit

In a knapsack or cardboard box, store a canteen, a flashlight, a compass, nature books, binoculars, a whistle, a walkie-talkie (pretend or real), a disposable camera, a water bottle, a magnifying glass, a hat, and boots.

Hair Salon Supplies
In a large box put a mirror, curlers, hair pins, a blow-dryer (toy or real with the cord cut off), combs, brushes, small towels, magazines, empty plastic shampoo bottles, emery boards, toy nail polish, play makeup, jewelry, a pencil, paper, play money, and an appointment book.

Painter's Kit
You can use a plastic bucket to store a hat (which you may find for free at a paint supply store), different-sized brushes, a paint roller, an old sheet for a drop cloth, a rag, and sandpaper. Your child can paint outdoors with water.

Fire Fighter's Equipment
This kit, which can be stored in a big cardboard box, can include a fire hat, a raincoat, boots, an old cut piece of garden hose, a pretend (or real) walkie-talkie, goggles, and gloves.

Doctor's Kit
In a plastic box, place cotton balls, a play thermometer, empty pill bottles, labels, paper, pens, an old white shirt, bandages, Band-Aids, plastic syringes, and a toy stethoscope. You can get some of these from your pediatrician.

Sets like these can also be made for police officers, scientists, nurses, shoe salespersons, grocers, astronauts, magicians, and waiters/waitresses. You can vary the contents as your child grows and changes.

Do coloring books limit creativity?

There are many kinds of coloring books available, such as cartoon books, educational books, animal books, and history books. They're all based on the same activity—a child colors a pre-drawn picture. Although this may seem enjoyable to an adult, a young child who spends time with coloring books may miss out on the chance to create his own artwork and know the enjoyment of drawing.

Parents sometimes buy these books because they think coloring within the lines will improve their child's hand-eye coordination. Yet so much of what a child does involves hand-eye coordination. When he picks up a raisin, puts together a puzzle, builds with blocks, or draws with a crayon on plain paper, he's improving his skills. He doesn't need a coloring book for practice.

Some parents believe that a child will learn to complete tasks if he works in a coloring book. But often, he's unable to successfully stay within the lines and becomes frustrated. A child between three and five may feel like a failure when he sees how "messy" his coloring looks. "I can't do this." And parents may be more critical of their child's work when the task is to color within the lines rather than to draw whatever he likes. Eventually, he may lose his interest in drawing and coloring: "I'm just not good at this."

Children are often given pre-done or partly completed artwork in nursery school or day care centers. They shouldn't then spend most of their arts and crafts time at home with pre-drawn coloring books. Parents should limit coloring books until their child is at least five or six years old. At that age, he will be better able to color within the lines and may find the activity more satisfying. But even then, the use of coloring books should be limited.

The best kind of artwork is the child's own. Your three- to five-year-old will enjoy using pens, pencils, markers (especially with fine tips), and crayons to color on blank paper. When your child has a chance to draw what he likes, the drawing will be a part of him, and his pictures of people, animals, boats, and so on will be unique. "Look what I made!" Of course, some children are more interested in arts and crafts than others, and some will show more skill. But all children enjoy drawing if they feel successful. And as one four-and-a-half-year-old said, "When you draw and draw, you get better."

Keep art supplies available so your child can draw and color when he wants to. If you have a variety of pens and pencils, he can pick the ones that are most comfortable to use. Many young children who have trouble drawing with crayons do much better with pens and markers.

Why does my child always say, "Watch me, Mom!"?

"Look! I'm jumping off the diving board." "Dad, watch me ride my bike." "Watch me do a cartwheel."

Children constantly ask their parents to pay attention. Even in the car, a child will ask a parent who's driving to look at a picture in his book or watch him make faces in the mirror. He doesn't think about what his parents are doing, only about his immediate desire to be watched. Sometimes these calls for attention are delightful. Sometimes they're annoying.

Your child does a lot of things he considers exciting, and he wants to share them with you. As he perfects a skill or tries something new, he wants to be acknowledged and praised. Kids thrive on attention and positive feedback from parents. They want to hear "Terrific," "Great job," "Nice throw," and "Good try." Since parents don't always pay attention spontaneously, children say, "Watch me!" again and again.

Parents often underestimate the importance of watching. When you pay attention, your child believes he's interesting and important enough to capture your attention, which helps him develop a healthy self-image.

You can learn a great deal about your child's interests and abilities by watching him participate in activities. However, you should be careful about offering unsolicited advice. When your child says, "Watch me," he wants approval, not coaching. One boy who used to say, "Watch me play baseball!" gradually lost interest because of his father's constant instructions. "Hold your glove like this. Lift your arm higher when you throw. Let me show you how to hit the ball." The boy's enjoyment faded because—whatever his father's real intentions—the boy heard only criticism. "I'm not good enough. Why keep trying?"

You may find that you're, like most adults, engrossed in your own activities. There are phone calls to make, emails to write, bills to pay, laundry to do, repairs to attend to. When you're occupied, you may not want to take time to watch your child perform some seemingly trivial activity. Yet childhood years go by quickly, and children's requests are reasonable and increasingly infrequent. A few minutes of acknowledgment and interest can enhance your child's view of himself and give you something to think about and remember. Once it's too late, many parents wish they'd spent more time "watching" when their children were young.

Should my child play with children his own age?

All young children, even those under a year old, love to be around other children. When children one and a half years old and younger play together, they usually get along well. They play side-by-side, independently engaged but enjoying each other's company, and there are few arguments over sharing. Occasional bickering passes quickly because children these ages can be easily distracted.

By the time children are two or three years old, however, play-time can be full of arguments for playmates of the same age. They struggle with each other over possessions, sharing, and autonomy, and constantly shout, "That's mine!" Parents often have a hard time watching children these ages play together. Young children don't pay attention to each other's needs and often don't give in without fighting. When children turn four they get along better, although there's often a streak of competitiveness and sometimes bossy behavior as each tries to exert power.

Play is generally much smoother when children of mixed ages play together. A group made up of two- to five-year-olds will struggle less because each child is at a different developmental stage with different needs. A younger child will watch and imitate an older one, asking for help with games and tasks, and getting information. An older child, who is less possessive, will give in to younger ones, offering help and leading games.

Although parents are usually comfortable when their young child plays with an older friend, they're not as sure when their older child plays with a younger one. Parents may feel that their child will be bored with younger children or will be brought down to their level. But a five-year-old playing with a three-year-old will challenge himself, depending on the activities he's involved in. He'll play elaborate games with the simple toys available, lead a complex game, or create his own arts and crafts projects. He might enjoy the chance to play again with toys he's outgrown. And he may feel good playing around younger children because he can be helpful and knowledgeable and direct his friends' play. "Let's put the blocks here and build a castle," "The puzzle piece goes there," or "Do you want to hold my hamster? Be gentle, he has fragile bones." His own confidence will be boosted when he can teach and lead.

Sometimes there are problems with mixed age groups. An older child may engage in elaborate play that the younger one doesn't understand, and both children may become frustrated. And some older children may feel compelled to boss a younger child. When such children (who are often reenacting what happens to them when they play with an older sibling or friend) sense they are bigger than the children they're playing with, they try to exert power. Parental supervision is needed in such situations to keep the play between younger and older children peaceful.

When you arrange playdates for your child, at times you may find it works best when he plays with children his own age; at other times you'll want him to practice relating to and accepting children of different ages. After all, in your family, in the neighborhood, and out in public, he's involved with people of all ages. What's more important than the ages of playmates is how well the children get along.

How can I encourage art at home?

The art projects kids do in school often aren't particularly creative. Teachers distribute pre-cut figures to be decorated, or tell the whole class to make identical orange pumpkins or Mayflower ships. Children are sometimes given coloring book-type sheets and told to color them in. Such work leaves little room for expression and creativity. If you want your child to have fun doing original artwork, you usually have to encourage it at home.

You can begin by providing a variety of appealing art materials: clay and sculpting compounds; candle wax and beeswax; an assortment of pens, pencils, paints, and markers; good quality paper, glue, and scissors; and popsicle sticks, small pieces of fabric and felt, wood chips, buttons, and glitter. These materials can be found at variety stores, hobby and art supply shops, and office supply stores.

If your child already has a preference for one medium, you can provide appropriate materials. A child who enjoys painting can be offered a table easel and paints of different sorts, including watercolors, acrylics, oil, and tempera. You can give her different-sized brushes, paper, and canvas.

The materials you buy should allow open-ended artwork. Coloring books, paint-by-number pictures, and pre-cut projects limit a child's creativity. Parents who want to encourage their child's free expression should avoid them.

Your child will be tempted to try new art materials if they're stored in an accessible place or set out in an appealing way. You can leave markers and paper on the kitchen table where your child will see them and be tempted to start drawing. You can reserve an accessible shelf, box, or drawer for art materials. You can also set aside space in your basement or elsewhere for large art projects and materials, such as easels. Your child will feel she has a special place for her big cardboard sculptures and creations made out of straws, papier-mâché, or clay.

One of the best places for working on smaller projects is the kitchen, since it's often the center of the home. While your child works, you can be nearby, ready to look at a new project or listen to her talk about her creation.

Some parents hesitate to encourage artwork at home because they fear a mess. However, table surfaces can easily be protected with newspaper or vinyl covers. A child can wear old clothes when she works, or cover her clothes with a smock. You shouldn't make cleanup a major issue. Your child may avoid artwork altogether if she knows she has to do a big cleanup when she's done.

How should I react to my child's artwork?

When your child's finished with an art project, compliment her work and avoid passing negative judgments. Let her artwork be enjoyable and free from criticism. Comment positively on her use of shape, design, and color. If you're sure of the subject of a drawing, say, "What a beautiful bird," or "That looks like a very fast car." If you're not sure, simply say, "Very nice. You spent a lot of time on that." You can also ask her to tell you about her art. "Where did you get your idea?" "How did you swirl the colors together?" "Tell me about your picture."

At times your child will be concerned about the success of her artwork. If a project doesn't turn out as she'd planned, she may feel frustrated and disappointed. Try to encourage her, and suggest ways her "mess-up" can be turned into something else.

Sometimes a younger sibling will give up on art if she decides her older brother or sister is better than she. Don't let this happen. Continue to provide materials, praise and encourage your child's attempts, and don't compare her to her siblings. Since most kids enjoy the sense of accomplishment finished artwork can bring, your child will most likely continue creating as long as you provide materials and let her know you appreciate her work.

Finally, encourage your child to do as much artwork as she likes. The more she draws, paints, and sculpts, the better she'll become and the better she'll feel about her creations.

Chapter 7

TRICKY SITUATIONS

- What should I tell my child about pregnancy and birth?
- When will my child no longer be afraid to have a haircut?
- Should I prepare my child for doctor's appointments?
- What should I tell my child about the dentist?
- Why is Halloween difficult for my child?
- How can I make Halloween less scary?
- What can I do about my child's fear of monsters?
- Why is my child afraid of Santa Claus?
- How can I help prepare my child for a visit to see Santa?
- What should I tell my child when everyone else has lost teeth?
- Should my child believe in the tooth fairy?
- How should I respond when my child says, "When I grow up, I'm going to be..."?
- Is it okay to give my son a doll or give my daughter a truck?
- Why does my child get anxious before holidays and her birthday?
- Will my five-year-old ever give up thumb-sucking?
- Why is my child so aggressive?
- How can I help my child control his behavior?

What should I tell my child about pregnancy and birth?

"Mommy, how did the baby get in your stomach?" "How did I get born?" "Am I going to have a baby, too?" You may be caught by surprise as your child begins asking questions about sex and childbirth. You may wonder how much to tell your child and when to tell her. Some books and specialists advise parents to give young children all the facts about sex and reproduction, but young children are unable to absorb and comprehend such information. Learning about and understanding reproduction is a gradual process that continues through the childhood years.

Young children have their own ideas about how the human body works, based on their observations and experience. Before you talk to your child about pregnancy, ask what she thinks so you'll know where to start the discussion. "How do you think the baby got inside of me?" Many children believe that eating too much causes pregnancy and that a woman gives birth in the same way she has a bowel movement. A child who's heard that a baby starts from a special seed might think that pregnancy comes from eating seeds. Parents may discover that their child is afraid of pregnancy, since children often fear things they don't understand and things they imagine.

Before you offer your child the facts about pregnancy and birth, wait for her to ask questions. There's no need to volunteer information if she's not yet curious about the subject. And when she does ask, don't overwhelm her with information. Start with simple explanations: "The baby grows in a special place inside the mother." Wait for her to ask for more before you continue your discussion; don't feel that you have to tell all the facts at one time.

If you do explain too much too soon, your child may become confused, frightened, or upset. One five-year-old girl, after hearing the details of childbirth, declared, "That's disgusting. I'm never going to have a baby." A three-and-a-half-year-old, who had been enrolled in a sibling childbirth class where he heard all the facts about birth, still believed, "Mom's stomach unzips so the baby can get out."

If your child seems curious about pregnancy and birth, explain the facts in simple terms that you think she can understand. "You grew inside mommy's tummy." "Doctors and nurses help when babies are ready to be born." "When the baby is big enough it comes out through a special passage in mommy's body." Don't put pressure on yourself to come up with the right words. Just keep it basic and simple, and satisfy your child's curiosity without overwhelming her. When she's older, she'll have an easier time understanding, cognitively and emotionally, the facts about pregnancy.

Talking about sex and pregnancy is naturally uncomfortable for many parents. However, it's not just explanations that teach your child about sex and intimacy. Throughout your child's life, she'll learn about relationships by watching the way you and your spouse treat each other. If you show each other respect and warmth, she'll become respectful and warm in her relationships as she grows. Those lessons can sometimes be more powerful than "the talk."

When will my child no longer be afraid to have a haircut?

It's hard to give haircuts to children under two because they wriggle around so much, and it's hard to cut the hair of children over two because they're often afraid of haircuts, and struggle and resist. Two- and three-year-olds often believe that haircuts hurt, that shampoo will get in their eyes and sting, and that they'll be helpless sitting in front of a stranger with scissors.

It might help to give your child a doll to play beauty shop with. As she washes and cuts (or pretends to cut) the doll's hair, she may begin to feel in control of a situation that frightens her.

If your child is very young or quite frightened of haircuts, you may want to cut her hair at home. You or a relative or close friend can do this as she sits in her high chair and plays with some of her toys or watches you in a mirror. Since it's hard for young children to hold still, you shouldn't expect your child's home haircut to be perfect.

When your child is three or four, you may want to take her to a professional stylist. For a first haircut, go to someone recommended by other parents or someone who specializes in cutting children's hair. Before you bring her in for an appointment, you might want to observe the stylist and talk to him or her about your child's anxiety.

Your child might feel comfortable going to the same barber shop or hair salon you use. She may have seen your stylist at work already, and be familiar with the surroundings and the people in the shop. Taking her with you when you (or your older child) get a haircut is a good way to help her get over her fears. If she resists professional haircuts but you're determined to take her to a stylist, let her sit on your lap during the haircut, distract her with an interesting object, or promise her a treat.

Should I prepare my child for doctor's appointments?

Many children have negative feelings—based on past experience and fearful imaginings—about seeing a doctor. If your child is afraid of doctors, you might be tempted to keep an appointment from him; you may even consider starting out for the office without letting him know where you both are going. Although this may seem like a good way to keep your child from getting upset, deceiving him is a mistake. You deprive him of time to prepare for the visit, and you may increase his fear. He might believe that you didn't tell him about the appointment because there was something to be afraid of. It's always better to let your child know in advance about an office visit.

If your child is under two years old, you may have a difficult time preparing him for the appointment. A child this young, who won't fully understand the reasons for his visit, may enter the doctor's office calmly and then cry or feel anxious when he goes into the examining room. Many parts of a standard checkup are uncomfortable: the child gags as his throat is checked, he feels momentary pain during blood tests and inoculations, he's measured and tested with cold instruments. No matter how well-mannered the physician is, the examination can be an unpleasant and therefore fearful experience.

During an examination, you can offer comfort and reassurance to your child: "I'm right here beside you," "I know you don't like to have your ears checked," or "The doctor's almost done." But such words may not relieve your child's anxiety, especially when, as sometimes happens, you're physically restraining him so the doctor can continue the examination. Sometimes a child in this situation will feel comforted if his toy or blanket is nearby.

You'll be more successful preparing your child if he's between three and five years old. He'll be better able to understand what happens during an exam and to verbalize some of his anxieties. Talk ahead of time about the appointment. Tell him briefly about the procedures, the instruments the doctor will use, the toys in the waiting room, and the setup of the examining rooms, but try to present this information in a way that won't frighten him: "Do you remember the table in the examining room? I can read you a story while you sit up there and wait for the doctor." "There are cups in the room so you can get a drink of water." If an injection is scheduled, say, "Your shot might hurt, but only for a minute."

When your child expresses his fears, accept them; don't pressure him to "be brave" or "be good." When he knows that he can say "ouch" or cry, he may feel less upset about getting an injection or having his ears and throat checked.

He may tell you he doesn't want to take his clothes off in the doctor's office. This is a common worry for children four to five years old. Let him know he may have to undress, but talk to your doctor about the situation. Many pediatricians will accommodate a modest child.

Your child may relieve some of his own anxiety about appointments by playing doctor. When he takes the role of doctor, he's in control as he re-experiences some of the uncomfortable and frightening things that have happened to him. Children usually play doctor by using a toy stethoscope, giving pretend injections, and using bandages.

When your child plays doctor with a friend, they may undress and examine each other. This is a common, innocent occurrence. Set limits about keeping clothes on, but don't make your child feel ashamed for playing this way.

No matter how well you prepare your child for a doctor's appointment, he may remain anxious and afraid. Some children are just more worried than others about appointments and doctors. As long as he's fearful, the best you can do is accept his feelings, give him honest information about what to expect, and offer him reassurance: "The doctor is going to help you feel better."

What should I tell my child about the dentist?

Because the mouth is a source of pleasure for a young child, when he feels discomfort or pain in his mouth, the experience can seem intolerable. Therefore, your child may strongly resist a visit to the dentist, even though he'll only feel mildly uncomfortable there.

Most children first go for a dental checkup when they're three or three and a half years old. A younger child will go if he has a problem with his teeth or gums. Although a child under three probably will not understand what a dental visit is about, you can still describe, in a simple way, the dentist's procedures: "He's going to look inside your mouth and check your teeth." At the office, your child might cooperate if he's examined while sitting on your lap. If this isn't possible, you should at least stay nearby so you can offer reassurance.

A child who's three or older is usually able to cooperate and follow directions well enough to be examined by a dentist. When your child's going for his first checkup, tell him what to expect. Try acting out a visit to the office if you think your child's fearful. You can read your child picture books about going to the dentist or call the office before the appointment and ask how to help your child feel less anxious.

Despite your preparations, your child may still enter the dentist's office feeling scared, and what he sees and hears there may make him feel worse. The sound of the drill can be frightening, and the dentist's instruments look sharp. When your child is sitting in the chair, he can feel vulnerable and afraid, since he doesn't have control over what goes into his mouth. Encourage him to express his feelings and ask the dentist questions: "Will that hurt me? When will you be done?" If you've chosen a dentist who's sensitive to children, he or she will reassure your child and explain the procedures in advance, and perhaps provide a mirror so your child can watch. You or the dentist might be able to distract your child by talking about the "treasure" he'll take home after the appointment.

It sometimes happens that parents are more afraid of dental exams than their children. If you're apprehensive about dentists, try not to pass your anxieties on to your child.

Why is Halloween difficult for my child?

Young children regard Halloween with a mixture of excitement and uneasiness. On the one hand, the holiday means candy, dressing up, and a full day of fun with friends, but on the other hand, it means strange sights, frightening sounds, and darkness. The ambivalence that children feel about the two sides of Halloween carries over to most aspects of the holiday, including anticipation, picking out costumes, and trick-or-treating. And parents have ambivalent feelings, too, about the issues of safety and eating sweets.

Before Halloween begins, some parents find that their child's behavior changes. She may become more silly or aggressive or may whine more than usual, asking again and again, "How many more days till Halloween?" Much of the difficulty before the holiday centers around her desire to wear her costume. If she's allowed to dress up in it before Halloween, she may have an easier time waiting for the enjoyable as well as the scary activities to begin. She may also feel less anxious if she can mark off the remaining days on a calendar or tear one piece of a paper chain off for each day left before October 31.

Some parents, as part of the pre-Halloween excitement, buy or borrow holiday books. Yet these books often have pictures and ideas that can frighten young children, who believe that what they see in a book is real. If a Halloween story is too frightening, change the words as you read, or try creating your own family Halloween picture books.

The most exciting part of Halloween is usually picking out and wearing a costume. Children like to dress up because they can experiment with fantasy and try out different roles: they can be television characters, princesses, superheroes, scary figures, or grown-up workers. It's very common for children to change their minds a few times about what they want "to be" for Halloween and argue about costume choices. In most cases, let your child choose her own costume.

Some children are afraid of costumes, especially ones designed to be frightening. Since young children don't fully understand the difference between reality and make-believe, they're not convinced that a scary ghost or a monster is only pretend. Even when they know the person under the disguise, they may respond to the costume with fear. When she sees a neighbor with a witch's mask, she believes the witch is real and is easily scared—in spite of your reassurances. When the mask is off, it's the neighbor she recognizes. When the mask goes back on, it's a witch. This is how young children think and reason.

Because of fear, your child may not want to dress up for Halloween. This may make you feel uneasy or embarrassed as you wonder why your child doesn't like Halloween when other children seem to. In this situation try to remember that all children are different—ones with older siblings may feel more comfortable in costumes, and outgoing children may enjoy dressing up more than reserved ones do. The age of a child makes a big difference, and older children, who are better able to understand that a real person is behind each mask, often enjoy holiday costumes more.

How can I make Halloween less scary?

If your child is afraid of costumes, you can try to reassure her by saying, "Costumes look scary, but they're only pretend. People pretend to be ghosts just like you pretend you're a fire fighter." Sometimes such statements work, but often they don't. If your child is afraid, and you've tried unsuccessfully to lessen her worries, don't pressure her. She'll grow out of her fears when she can understand what's real and what's not.

Sometimes a child will wear a costume but not a mask. Masks partially cover a child's eyes and face, and this may intensify a child's fears. Try using face makeup instead of a mask, or help your child make a mask that she can hold rather than wear. Such a mask will let her exert quick control and may make her feel more comfortable.

When Halloween night comes and most children's costumes are on, the trick-or-treating begins. Your child may find this to be a difficult part of the holiday. It's dark and there are many people outside, all looking like strangers, many looking very spooky. A child who finds costumes frightening may be overwhelmed by the sight of so many disguised trick-or-treaters.

Your child may be afraid to trick-or-treat at other people's homes. All year long you've told her not to talk to strangers, and you and your child don't go to unfamiliar houses. Yet on Halloween night it's suddenly acceptable to go and ask for candy. A neighbor's house may seem strange if your child has never been inside. And your child may be afraid either that people will answer their doors wearing scary costumes or that she'll have to stand at a doorstep with other children dressed in frightening disguises.

Your two- or three-year-old may hesitate to trick-or-treat because she's never done it before. And if your child is shy, she may not want to talk to neighbors, even if you coach her, "Now say, 'Trick-or-treat.'" Many children don't like to be focused on by people who admire their costumes. "Oh, look at the cute bunny! Who's under there?"

There's another side to trick-or-treat anxiety—your concerns about your child's safety. Because of frightening news stories, many parents warn their children about unwrapped candy and spend time looking through their children's bags for open or suspicious candy. In order to avoid the possibility of unsafe candy, some parents decide to skip trick-or-treating altogether, instead trying community parties, costume parades, home parties, or Halloween craft treats.

If you allow trick-or-treating, you'll have to decide what to do with all the candy. You might try letting your child eat a few pieces on Halloween night or letting her eat whatever she wants. The days following the holiday can be challenging if your child doesn't lose interest in her candy. If you want to eventually throw the goodies out, let your child know ahead of time, with the understanding that the candy really belongs to her. Let her pick out some pieces to save, realizing the work she did to get the candy and considering her feelings. Through all of this it might help you to realize that, while Halloween can be an exciting time, it's not always easy for young children.

What can I do about my child's fear of monsters?

All children have fears. They worry about monsters in their closets, alligators under their beds, or "scary ghosts" at their windows. Such frightening images are part of a child's internal world. And bedtime darkness makes a child feel even more scared and vulnerable.

The specific scary images that frighten a child can be introduced by a TV show, a movie, a fairy tale, or even a picture in a book. Some parents who try to alleviate their child's fears by showing him a book about nice monsters may actually be giving their child something else to be afraid of. This can happen because he has difficulty distinguishing what's real from what's not. Once a child sees a picture of a monster, even a harmless one, he may be convinced that such a thing exists. Therefore, parents may want to keep a sensitive child from seeing scary books, television shows, or movies.

If your child tells you he's afraid of monsters, understand that his fears are real. He really believes monsters exist. Try reassuring him: "Sometimes children think that monsters are real, but I know there are no such things." But be careful not to pressure your child into agreeing that his fears are irrational. And don't dismiss his fears by saying, "Don't be afraid." Children who are told their fears are silly will continue to feel afraid but may not openly express themselves, because they anticipate being ridiculed or shamed. Instead, they may cry, cling, or have frequent scary dreams.

Try to get your child to express his fears, since talking can help him deal with them. The inability to discuss fears can make them feel more real and give them more power. Ask your child, "What does a monster do? What does it look like? Can you draw a picture of it? Where did you think you saw it?" Such questions will help you learn more about what frightens your child. When he's scared, you'll probably have to spend more time comforting and reassuring him at bedtime. Children's fears are what bring them into their parents' bed. They feel better when their parents are close by. You may feel more patient about this if you remember your own childhood fears. Although you may have received assurance from your parents, you probably still believed that frightening things lurked in the closets and under your bed.

It should help to know that as your child grows, he'll develop the ability to tell what's real from what isn't, which will help many of his fears fade. In the meantime, patience and understanding will get you and your child through this phase.

Why is my child afraid of Santa Claus?

A beautifully dressed two-year-old waits in line to see Santa Claus. When it's her turn, Santa says, "Come here, little girl," and the girl's parents say, "Go sit on his lap." She listens, looks at the smiling face in front of her, and bursts into tears. She's afraid of Santa.

It often surprises parents to learn that many children fear such a friendly character. After all, from a parent's perspective, Santa represents kindness and the spirit of gift giving. When your child resists sitting on Santa's lap, you may become embarrassed and easily wonder, "What's wrong with my child?" You may try to force her to sit on Santa's lap or use bribes. "If you sit on Santa's lap, you'll get toys for Christmas." Even when parents are patient, they can be unsuccessful in getting their young child to come in contact with

Santa. Young children struggle and resist him out of fear, and it's almost impossible to convince them not to be afraid.

Most children under the age of five believe that what they hear and see is real. They regard their own perspectives as absolute and for them, Santa is real. They see him in shopping malls, they read and sing about him, and their parents talk as though he truly exists.

Santa, with a rather deep voice and a beard that covers most of his face, can be scary-looking to a young child. Since a child's in contact with Santa only during the Christmas season, he's unfamiliar. Children don't go to unfamiliar people with ease. A young child's not sure Santa's nice, and parents aren't always reassuring about his looks. While you tell your child that a Halloween character or a clown is only someone dressed in a costume, you don't say that Santa, too, is wearing a costume. You don't want your child to know.

A young child's belief in a real Santa can take on a mysterious quality, giving Santa tremendous power. Santa "knows" when she's good or bad, and he decides what gifts she'll receive. He seems omnipotent, flying through the sky, entering her home when she's asleep, watching her all the time.

A child may worry about being judged by Santa, who will decide if she's been good enough to get gifts on Christmas. And parents, not realizing their child's already under a lot of pressure during this time of the year, may say, "You'd better be good, or Santa won't bring you presents." Parents often use this line when they're frustrated with their child's behavior, but it adds a threatening note to the fun and excitement of Christmas. A child who hears this threat repeatedly may become anxious, silly, aggressive, or fearful.

Realistically, young children can't live up to Santa's (or her parents') expectations of constant good behavior. Young children struggle when they have to pick up their toys, they don't like to go to bed, they usually don't brush their teeth or wash their hands and faces without being reminded (at least twice), and they don't always share, clean up, or help with day-to-day chores. It's not that children are "bad," it's that parents' and Santa's expectations are unrealistic.

Given Santa's power to judge, his unusual appearance, and his ability to see and be everywhere, it's not surprising when a young child has ambivalent feelings about approaching him. Your child wants to tell Santa what to bring for Christmas, and she wants to please you, but she's afraid.

How can I help prepare my child for a visit to see Santa?

Fortunately, if your child fears Santa, there are things you can do ahead of time to help her feel better. The most important is to reassure and prepare her by talking about Santa, mentioning his size, voice, and clothes. You can explain that he's friendly and likes talking with children about Christmas. You can also try having your child go up to Santa with a sibling or friend. Be selective about the Santas you visit, asking your friends about their experiences at various shopping centers, and watching a Santa to see how he acts with young children. A Santa who doesn't put too much pressure on children will make you and your child more comfortable.

Finally, consider your child's age and personality. A shy child might display more apprehension. A one-and-a-half- or two-year-old will be more frightened than a three- or four-year-old. And children with confident older siblings can often be convinced that Santa's nice and likes children.

Whatever you try, your child may still cry, not want to look at Santa, or refuse to sit on his lap. However, be reassured, that in a year or so there'll be changes in your child's attitude, and even though she may cry this year, she'll probably have fun visiting Santa next Christmas.

What should I tell my child when everyone else has lost teeth?

Losing a first tooth is a milestone. From kindergarten on, children look forward to the event as a sign that they're truly growing up. Parents often forget how important the experience is and how hard it can be when their child is one of the last in his group to have a loose tooth.

If your child is upset because he has "slow teeth," spend time listening to him and reassuring him. Even though his problem is a mild one, don't lightly dismiss his unhappiness, because his feelings are very real. He wants to experience what his friends and classmates have gone through. If he has older siblings, he's seen them get money or a gift along with a lot of attention for losing teeth. It's natural that he wants to be part of this.

Your child may have a kindergarten or first grade teacher who makes a fuss over lost teeth. Some classrooms have colorful wall charts showing how many teeth each student has lost, and some teachers offer special privileges on the day a tooth comes out. If your child is unhappily waiting for his first loose tooth, such school activities may make him feel worse.

Fortunately, you can promise him that he'll lose a tooth. While you wait, you can read him some comforting books about other children in his situation. One mother wrote soothing notes to her child, saying that the tooth fairy knew all about him and would be visiting one day. Other parents suggest that their child wiggle their front teeth, looking for a hint of movement. Even if it takes months for a tooth to fall out, a child will feel better as soon as he detects a bit of looseness.

Occasionally the first tooth a child loses is one a dentist extracts. If your child has to go through this procedure because of dental problems, talk to him about what will happen. If he's anxious, let the dentist know, and ask for help in reassuring your child. If your child wants you close by during the extraction, plan to stay with him. However, if you anticipate an outburst, you might want to send him off with just the dentist and assistant. Some children are more in control of their emotions when their parents aren't with them.

Before and after the tooth is pulled, tell your child about the "treasure" he'll get at the dentist's office and the surprise he'll find under his pillow. Even though an extraction can be unpleasant, when it's done, he'll still have the excitement of having lost his first tooth.

Should my child believe in the tooth fairy?

Young children generally follow their parents' lead when it comes to believing in imaginary characters. If parents encourage their child to believe the tooth fairy is real, she's likely to go along with them. And if parents tell their child there's no such thing as the tooth fairy, she'll probably accept that as fact.

Of course, your child may figure the truth out on her own, especially if she's awake when you put money under her pillow. "Dad, I saw you! You're the tooth fairy!" Some kids hear the truth from older siblings. However, having older siblings can sometimes make a child believe more firmly, since tooth fairy visits have been part of their household lore from a child's early years.

Children often ask each other, "Do you believe in the tooth fairy?" While they may take different positions, they rarely quarrel about the issue. Instead they'll say, "Carlos believes in the tooth fairy, but I know it's my parents," or "Emma doesn't believe in the tooth fairy, but I do!"

Children who believe in the tooth fairy sometimes worry about getting the rituals right. If a child's misplaced her tooth at school or at a friend's house, or if she didn't notice it fall out (or swallowed it), she may be afraid the tooth fairy won't visit. Another common fear is that she won't get to keep the tooth; many children are interested in their teeth and don't want to give them up to the tooth fairy.

When your child has one of these concerns, let her know she'll get a gift under her pillow whether the tooth is there or not. If you want her to continue believing in the tooth fairy, suggest that she leave the fairy a message explaining the special circumstances.

At some point your child may ask, "Are you the tooth fairy?" Ask her what she thinks. If she really knows the truth, explain that you are, and then add, "It was fun to pretend a fairy was leaving you gifts," or "I liked thinking about the tooth fairy when I was little, and I thought you would too."

If you choose not to teach your child to believe in the tooth fairy, you and your child can still have fun with the idea. You can pretend the fairy is real, and you can leave your child funny notes "from the fairy." If you don't want to talk of a fairy at all, you can leave a special treat "from Mom and Dad" under her pillow.

Magical thinking slowly disappears during the elementary years, and eventually all children realize the tooth fairy isn't real. Still, the myth is an enjoyable one whether your child believes or just plays along. Getting a treat—money, stickers, or a small toy—makes losing a tooth even more special.

How should I respond when my child says, "When I grow up, I'm going to be..."?

"I'm going to be a basketball player." "I'm going to be a princess." "I'm going to be president."

Young children see unlimited possibilities. Their thinking is magical, and they believe they'll accomplish whatever they desire. All children, when asked, "What do you want to be when you grow up?" give an answer based on their immediate interests and experience.

Kids don't think the way an adult does. They can't put themselves in the place of someone who's worked hard to accomplish a goal. They don't think about obstacles, expenses, time, or limited abilities. Instead, they have an innocent optimism that leads to dramatic conclusions. "When I grow up, I'm going to be a star!"

When your child tells what he's going to be when he grows up, don't feel you have to set him straight. Respect your child's confident statements, and try to learn more about his interests and thinking. If he says he's going to be a spaceman, ask, "What will you do in space?" One five-year-old said he was going to build a "Kids' World Park" when he grows up so "kids can play all the time."

Childhood is short. Through the years, your child will discover his own limitations and learn how the world really works. His innocence will gradually fade as he comes to terms with life's realities. You do him no harm by encouraging him, taking an interest in what he says, and listening to his big dreams.

Is it okay to give my son a doll or give my daughter a truck?

There are toys that all children use—balls, puzzles, blocks, clay, crayons, board games—and there are "boy" toys and "girl" toys. Some parents try to avoid stereotyped or sexist toys and allow their children to choose playthings from the full range available. But some parents are uncomfortable when their children play with non-traditional toys. These parents, who do not buy cars and action figures for their girls or baby strollers and tea sets for their boys, fear that playing with toys intended for the opposite sex weakens a child's identification with his or her own sex.

Some parents may discourage their daughter when she acts like a "tomboy" or shows an interest in aggressive, supposedly masculine toys. But parents who pressure their child to follow traditionally feminine pursuits may limit her potential.

Parents of boys can also restrict their child's development by demanding only masculine activities. Nursery-school and day care teachers often hear parents tell their sons that the classroom's house-keeping area is "just for girls." Yet there's nothing wrong with a boy who wants to play house or dolls. Boys need to learn how to nurture, just as girls do, and an interest in playing house is normal.

Some parents who don't mind if their children play with non-traditional toys still feel uncomfortable buying such toys. One mother was pleased that her son played with dolls at his friend's house, but couldn't bring herself to get him a doll when he asked. Similarly, a parent didn't mind her daughter's use of war toys in the neighborhood but resisted buying her a tank of her own.

Some parents who have children of both sexes encourage their sons and daughters to share toys, thus allowing non-traditional play. Other parents buy each sibling a few toys intended for the opposite sex so that brothers and sisters can play well together. One little girl had her own set of mini cars to use whenever her brother's play-mates came to the house. She joined in their games, and her parents avoided the struggles that come when one child is excluded.

When a child is under the age of three, he or she may be attracted to toys of interest to both sexes, but by the time children are three or four, they clearly identify which toys "belong" to which sex. One four-year-old girl noticed a two-and-a-half-year-old boy wearing nail polish and she began to question him about his interests: "Do you like Barbie? Do you like robots?" When he answered yes to both questions, she turned to her mom and said, "He's girlish-boyish."

Parents who encourage their child to play with whatever toys he or she likes—regardless of sex stereotypes—are often surprised when their child chooses the traditional "girl" or "boy" toys anyway.

Girls are drawn to dolls, toy houses, and dressing up, while boys are attracted to cars, superheroes, and space toys. Girls enjoy playing baby and house; boys like playing pirates, fire fighters, and spacemen. And all children become familiar with the "girl aisle" and the "boy aisle" in toy stores.

Certainly the media has a powerful influence. Advertisers clearly market their toys for a particular sex, and children rarely have a chance to see non-traditional play on commercials. But even considering the influence of television, children seem to have their own innate interests in typical, traditional play.

Given this strong drive girls have to play with "girl" toys and boys with "boy" toys, there's no need to worry if your child shows an interest in toys for the opposite sex. And there's no reason not to buy non-traditional toys if your child wants them.

In rare cases, parents might observe that their child seems particularly dissatisfied with his or her gender. A child who consistently tries to play and act like a member of the opposite sex may sense his or her parents' disappointment ("I wish he'd been a girl!"), may be reacting to family stress, or may be influenced by genetic factors. If you're concerned about your child's behavior, keep an eye on the situation, and in later years seek additional information and guidance on gender issues.

Why does my child get anxious before holidays and her birthday?

"How long 'til my birthday?" "When is three weeks up?" "Is it Halloween yet?" Parents hear such questions whenever special occasions approach. Children have a hard time waiting, and since their concept of time is different from an adult's, they ask about holidays over and over again. Parents can tell their excited child that Christmas is four weeks away and almost immediately, she'll ask again, "How long 'til Christmas?"

Young children begin anticipating a holiday as soon as preparations begin. Her day care or nursery-school class might make valentines weeks in advance, and her friends might discuss Halloween costumes long before October. Christmas preparations sometimes begin before Thanksgiving, giving children a great deal of time to watch holiday commercials, see store decorations going up, and think about presents.

When there's a long period of anticipation before a special event, children sometimes get anxious and excited, and may go through some behavior changes, becoming sillier, more active, and more likely to whine. Children who are admonished to "be good" in order to get birthday or Christmas gifts may feel pressured and become more aggressive. It's very hard under any circumstances for a child to be consistently good, and when she's anxiously anticipating a holiday, behaving well is that much harder. Some parents find that their child's behavior improves if they ease up on the holiday pressure, perhaps giving a surprise treat ("Just because I love you") to slow the build up.

You can try to help your child deal with the waiting period by giving her a calendar to mark off or by making a special paper chain. Each day for a week or two, your child can tear off one chain; the day all the chains are gone is the day she's been waiting for. These devices help some children stay calm, but generally children remain very excited. Be patient with your child's excitement and expect that your child will continually want the celebration to begin "now." You can sympathize if you consider your own feelings before special parties or vacations.

Your child may get particularly worked up before her birthday. Since party preparations take time, you may start planning her birthday weeks before the date, while your child considers who to invite and what presents she'd like. She may be very excited about the gifts and party, or she may have mixed feelings about being the center of attention and may decide, as one five-year-old did, "Nobody should sing 'Happy Birthday' to me at my party." Although there's no way to keep your child from feeling excited and anxious before her birthday, if you anticipate her feelings, you'll be more patient and better able to focus positively on her excitement.

Will my five-year-old ever give up thumb-sucking?

As children get older, it gets harder to accept some of their habits. Thumb-sucking in particular bothers many parents who find it embarrassing and frustrating. While you probably tolerated thumb-sucking earlier on, you may believe it's now inappropriate.

A three- or four-year-old who sucks his thumb probably does so less often than he once did. This is partly because he's now occupied with school, after-school activities, and friends. Most children these ages are inclined to suck their thumbs in private or when they're with family members.

Even though thumb-sucking decreases with age, most parents of a four- or five-year-old want their child to give up the habit completely. Some may argue with their child over thumb-sucking and end up in power struggles. Some parents back off for a while, and others give up in frustration, at a loss for what to do.

There are a number of reasons a four- or five-year-old sucks his thumb. It may be a well-established habit he hasn't felt pressured to break, or he may not be emotionally ready to stop. He may suck his thumb at night to help him fall asleep. If he feels insecure at school, he may seek comfort through thumb-sucking, or he may do it when he faces family situations he can't control, such as sibling rivalry, divorce, or constant tension.

Sometimes a four- or five-year-old gives up thumb-sucking in response to teasing and peer pressure. "Ooh, you still suck your thumb. That's for babies! I stopped sucking my thumb when I was two!" However, a child with a strong thumb-sucking habit may not respond at all to negative comments or care if other people watch him.

To help your child give up thumb-sucking, ask your child, "How can we help you stop sucking your thumb?" Remember that, while thumb-sucking is a problem for you, it may not seem like one to him.

You can suggest that your child wear a bandage on his thumb to remind him not to suck, or you can gently signal him when he puts his thumb in his mouth. This is more effective than abruptly pulling on his hand or angrily saying, "Take your thumb out of your mouth!"

Try distractions that occupy his hands—playing with play dough or helping in the kitchen. Avoid having him watch TV or do other activities where he's likely to suck his thumb. Reduce the amount of stress he's exposed to. Don't shame or ridicule him. It takes time to give up a habit, especially one that's so satisfying.

You might want to work out an agreement. If he stops sucking his thumb, he gets a reward. One family kept a daily chart for their daughter, and after a week of checkmarks for not sucking her thumb, she got a special game.

As you help your child give up his habit, create an atmosphere of respect in your home, and try to keep him from feeling humiliated or embarrassed because of his thumb-sucking. Don't let your other children make fun of him. If he seems particularly anxious, he may be feeling too pressured. You might want to slow down your attempts to eliminate his habit, or hold off for a few weeks.

Throughout this process, give lots of positive feedback. "You're really trying hard." Don't be surprised if steps forward are followed by steps backward. It's not easy for your child to give up thumb-sucking, especially if the initiative is yours and not his.

Why is my child so aggressive?

Aggression during childhood is challenging to deal with. Parents worry if their child is belligerent, offensive to others, and consistently rough. It is essential that you watch and carefully control your child's aggressive behaviors.

First, you should clearly and firmly let your child know what is and isn't appropriate. Your child will not know how to act if you send inconsistent and confusing messages. Don't excuse his aggression by saying, "Oh, that's just how boys act," or "At least he doesn't hide his feelings." Such attitudes don't teach your child that his negative behaviors are unacceptable.

Instead of being ambiguous, consistently let your child know that fighting, hitting, and using mean words is unacceptable. "I absolutely won't allow you to behave that way." State the consequences of negative behavior so your child knows what to expect. "If you treat Nick roughly, you'll have to come inside."

It's also important to find the source of your child's aggression. He may be copying behavior he is subjected to at home. He may fight with his siblings or peers because he's imitating you or to alleviate his feelings of fear, anger, and helplessness. And if he feels (from his point of view) that you don't give him enough attention or listen to his feelings, he may act out his frustration in aggressive ways.

Some children are aggressive due to problems at school or because they generally feel inferior. They attack others to feel more powerful. Siblings sometimes fight because they think they're being treated unfairly or because their parents actually do treat them in ways that encourage aggression, perhaps by favoring one or belittling another. The roots of aggression are sometimes difficult to find.

However, if you give your child more positive and playful attention at home, have realistic expectations for his age, praise him, nurture his interests, and set more consistent limits, aggressive behaviors will diminish. If aggressive behavior continues over a long period, you may need the guidance of a parenting coach or counselor.

How can I help my child control his behavior?

In most cases, positive action taken by you is enough to help your child control his behavior. You can offer him alternative ways to release his aggressive feelings and become a better role model for him.

Talk to him about acceptable ways to express his feelings. "When you're angry enough to hit your brother, you have to let him know with words, not actions. Tell him what's making you mad." "If you feel yourself getting so mad, don't hit—come to me for help."

Let your child see how you handle aggressive feelings in your own life. Show him how you talk out your problems or take time to cool off until you feel calm. Don't spank, grab his arm, or put him roughly in his car seat when you're angry or frustrated. Kids imitate their parents and, if you can model appropriate behavior, he'll learn from you.

Watch as he interacts with others. He may be aggressive in a playful way, tugging on a friend's shirt, teasing, pretending to be in a wrestling match, or calling out silly names. If the aggression seems benign, don't interfere. But such behavior can often escalate, and even if the tone stays playful, your child's aggression can become very annoying to others. If you see that happening, firmly step in: "Suzanne doesn't want you to push her like that."

Since explanations and talking about other children's feelings don't usually work with young children, give constant reminders. "You may not play roughly." "No hitting." Distract your child and his friends with a new activity or different topic of conversation. "Come in for a snack," "Show Brett your new game," or "Let's make a fort."

Your child simply may not yet have all the inner controls to halt his aggressive behavior. Until he acquires control, he'll need you to offer guidelines and be clear about how to treat others.

Chapter 8 GROWING INDEPENDENCE

- Why does my five-year-old still have trouble at bedtime?
- Why isn't my child more responsible?
- Will moving to a new home be difficult for my child?
- How can I help my child adjust to moving to a new home?
- Is it normal for my child to speak rudely to me when he's angry?
- How can I enhance my child's self-image?
- Am I over-scheduling my kindergarten child?
- How do I choose the best day camp for my child?

Why does my five-year-old still have trouble at bedtime?

Many parents believe that five-year-olds should go to bed on their own without arguing, and when their own child doesn't, they feel frustrated. They get tired of saying, "Brush your teeth," and "Now put on your pajamas." They're also bothered if their child dawdles or gets up once she's been put to bed.

Independent bedtime habits develop slowly. Most five-year-old children can fall asleep without having their parents stay with them, and many can take care of their middle-of-the-night needs: going to the bathroom, getting a drink, or finding an extra blanket. However, it's still common for five-year-olds to need help at bedtime. Many require prodding at night, and some don't get ready at all unless their parents guide them through almost every step of the process. All these reminders are necessary because children have a hard time separating themselves from their activities. They'd much rather continue playing or watching TV. And because bedtime is of no interest to them, they're easily distracted and need to be kept on track. The procrastination that bothers so many parents is the result of the young child's inability to focus on something she doesn't want to do.

Children this age still need their parents for bedtime rituals, which continue to be important. Some kids can't go to sleep without a story, a conversation, or a hug and a kiss. In busy families or on rushed days, bedtime may be the only time parents and children have quiet contact.

While most children need some parental help at night, if your child has consistent trouble at bedtime, try to find out why. There might be a simple explanation. Perhaps she's hungry and needs a snack in the evening. She may avoid bedtime because she's afraid of imaginary creatures or the dark and wants to put off going to sleep as long as possible. If that's the case, spend fifteen minutes or so in her room while she falls asleep, try keeping a light on at night, or suggest that she sleep with a personal treasure or newly received gift. She may also sleep more securely in a room shared with a sibling. She may also need less prodding if she falls asleep in your bed or if she knows that she can climb into your bed in the middle of the night.

Your child may have trouble because she simply isn't tired. Some parents, understandably eager for their child to get enough sleep for school or for time alone in the evenings, set bedtimes without considering their child's actual sleep needs. If you know that your child isn't sleepy, have her go to bed a little later, and be more flexible on weekends.

If her bedtime problems seem to be just habitual, you'll have to set limits and tell her the consequences of too much dawdling. "If you don't get ready quickly, you won't have time to play before bed." "When you take so long to get in bed, I don't have time to read to you." It's important to anticipate evening struggles rather than let annoyances build up to an angry battle of wills. It's also important to help your child bring her day to a pleasant close. Tell her something exciting that's coming up, and remind her of how special she is.

You can also try rewarding your child for getting ready on time. "If you're in bed in five minutes, I'll let you listen to a CD before you fall asleep." One child would get ready quickly in order to hear favorite stories about her family.

Bedtime will be less stressful if you try to be patient and remember that your child will gradually assume her own bedtime responsibilities. Meanwhile, as long as she responds to your reminders and does get ready for bed, you don't have to worry or feel defeated.

Why isn't my child more responsible?

All parents want their children to be responsible. They want them to be considerate of others, do their schoolwork carefully and on time, take care of pets, follow safety rules, and clean up. When children don't act responsibly, parents become frustrated. "When will he ever learn to do the right thing?"

It's helpful to know that responsibility is tied to a number of other traits, such as thoughtfulness, common sense, generosity, and empathy. Responsibility requires maturity, alertness, and a social conscience. A child under the age of five or six is too young to consistently show responsible traits and too young to consistently think about the consequences of his actions.

In order to become responsible, your child needs good role models. You set the standards your child will gradually follow. If you emphasize the importance of doing a good job and caring about others, your child will pick that up.

The process of learning to be responsible is neither quick nor smooth. Three- to five-year-olds need many reminders, particularly about picking up their toys. Since a child rarely enjoys or cares about this task, he isn't motivated to put his toys away.

Kids also don't understand the reasons for many tasks. Even when parents explain why jobs are necessary, their child might resist. "Why should I put the game away? Shannon took it out."

You may feel less frustrated if you accept that constant reminders are a necessary part of teaching your child to be responsible. Reminders are important in all areas of responsibility. Children need to be told about safety, consideration for others, sharing, cleanup, and schoolwork. For some responsibilities, a chart might be useful. Each day, a child checks off the jobs he's completed. Even with a chart, though, most kids still need reminders. Young children just can't consistently keep track of too many obligations.

If your child continually fails to be as responsible as you'd like, re-examine your expectations. You might be asking him to do too much. Try eliminating one or two of the less important tasks he struggles with, and see if he doesn't become more responsible about the remaining obligations. Also, be sure to leave him free time to play and pursue creative projects; if he has to spend a big portion of his time on tasks that don't interest him, he'll be too frustrated to do his best.

In teaching responsibility, as in many other aspects of parenting, you'll find your child becomes most cooperative when you get involved. Help him straighten his room, or offer to trade jobs so he can water the lawn while you pick up the toys.

If your child's able to behave somewhat responsibly after you've given him reminders, he's on the right track. Although you may wish he'd learn more quickly, be assured that as he grows, you'll continue to see progress as long as you patiently continue to reinforce responsible behavior at home.

Will moving to a new home be difficult for my child?

Moving can be exciting. It can also be stressful. There are upheavals, physical work, and sad separations for the whole family. As parents pack up toys, photographs, and clothes, they often feel nostalgic. As a child says good-bye to his room, his favorite play spots, and his friends, he may feel anxious and uncertain.

The success of a move depends on the circumstances involved. Families moving because of divorce, unexpected job transfer, job loss, illness, or death, face pressures and burdens not shared by those moving under happier circumstances. A family moving to a familiar neighborhood will have an easier time than one going to a strange city or state.

Parents' attitudes greatly influence the success of a move, since a child will often adopt their viewpoints as his own. If you're cheerful about going to a new home, your child will accept inevitable changes more easily than if you're nervous and upset.

The move will go more smoothly if your child doesn't have to change schools or day care. If he can spend his school hours with familiar teachers and friends, he can concentrate on the fun things about his new home: a playroom, a nearby park, or a hill to run down. Some parents who make a mid-school-term move to a community nearby let their child finish the year in his old school or child-care center. That way, he can be comfortable in class and still meet new neighborhood children.

Because parents get caught up in the physical demands of moving, they often don't take time to reassure and support their child. They may believe all kids are resilient and have an easy time adjusting. "You'll make lots of new friends." "Kindergarten is the same no matter where you go." Yet leaving familiar surroundings can upset any child.

How can I help my child adjust to moving to a new home?

The best way you can help your child is by spending more time with him, and listening to him talk and ask questions about the move. If he can express his fears, anger, and sadness, he'll feel better. If he believes his negative feelings are unacceptable, he'll hide them and express his anxiety in other ways. He may lose his appetite, whine, cry frequently, or fight more with his siblings.

Encourage your child to talk about moving. Ask questions. "What's the best part about moving? What don't you like?" "What can I do to make this easier for you?" Show that you understand his feelings. "I know it's hard to leave our house. You'll really miss your friends, won't you?" Talk about the separations he'll experience if you're moving far away. He may be upset about leaving grandparents, cousins, a babysitter, or teacher. Let him know he can stay in contact with people who are special to him. If he's four or five, help him plan a farewell with his friends by having his friends over for a party or outdoor snacks and games. He may decide to make cards for friends or offer them a treasure from his room.

Before you pack, take photographs or videos of each room in your house, and ask your child if he wants to be in the pictures. He might want to help with the packing, or he may want nothing to do with the process. Don't insist on his help. As you pack his belongings, don't get rid of his things without asking him. He may still feel attached to playthings he's outgrown, and if the move is difficult for him, he may not want to part with any possessions. "I'm keeping everything!" If he feels this way, put all the items you'd like to discard in a box, take them to the new house, and, after he's adjusted, ask which ones he'd like to keep.

Immediately after the move, resume important family rituals like bedtime stories, evening snacks, and breakfast with the whole family. If he's going to a new kindergarten class, show him his new school, and set up an appointment to visit the principal and tour the building. And remember, in the midst of unpacking, your child will need extra time, reassurance, and love.

Is it normal for my child to speak rudely to me when he's angry?

"Be quiet, Dad. You never let me do anything!" "I don't like you." "You're not fair! Leave me alone!"

When a child is allowed to spontaneously express his anger, he may say rude, hurtful things, because he's too young to consider his parents' feelings. In the heat of the moment, he says what he's thinking, and he doesn't understand adult reasoning.

Anger at parents is a normal part of growing up. Learning how to express negative feelings in socially acceptable ways takes time. It also takes patience on the part of parents. Yet many parents react harshly. "Don't you dare talk to me that way!" "I don't want to hear that tone of voice." If parents overreact toward their child for his disrespectful words, he may learn that feeling angry is bad and that angry thoughts shouldn't be spoken.

While some parents overreact, others feel helpless when faced with outbursts. "Should we allow this behavior?" "Why does he talk this way?" "Am I setting enough limits?" Many parents grew up with strong restrictions on their speech. "Don't ever say that again. It's not nice." They may be reluctant to impose similar restrictions on their child's expressions of anger, yet they feel uncomfortable listening to him say things they would never have said as children.

Your child needs a chance to speak his angry thoughts, but you also need to put limits on how he expresses himself. If certain words or attitudes are unacceptable to you, tell him. "It's all right for you to be mad at me, but you'll have to change your tone of voice." "When you stop name-calling, I'll be happy to listen to you." "I don't like it when you talk to me that way." "You'll have to find another way to tell me about being angry." Not only do such statements guide him toward better ways of expressing anger, but they demonstrate a respectful way of communicating that you'd eventually like him to adopt.

As you help him control the way he speaks to you, consider his age; a young child lacks communication skills. Also, remember that your child is greatly influenced by your behavior. If you expect him to speak respectfully, offer examples. Don't say, "Get over here this minute!" "Stop acting like a baby." "You better listen to me!" Instead, talk to him and treat him as you would like him to treat others.

With patience, limits, and guidance, he'll gradually learn to express most of his feelings appropriately. However, if you become concerned that he can't control his anger, consider seeking outside help, such as a parenting class. The way you treat this issue now will set the tone for communication with your child later.

How can I enhance my child's self-image?

Parents spend a great deal of time worrying about being consistent ("Should I always enforce family rules? Should I give in after I've said no?"), but there's really only one thing you have to be absolutely consistent about—letting your child know he's loved, valued, and important. A child who grows up hearing that message will develop a healthy self-image.

Parents can't compromise when it comes to giving their child feedback about his basic nature and worth. A child needs to hear again and again that his parents accept him as he is, with his strengths and weaknesses, personality, interests, and appearance. Parents should encourage their child to feel good about himself and his capabilities.

That doesn't mean you shouldn't show anger and disappointment when your child misbehaves. You have to set limits and tell your child what you expect. In fact, when you do set limits, you let him know you care a great deal about him and the way he acts.

However, there's a big difference between expressing disapproval of misbehavior and expressing general disapproval of a child. For whatever reasons, some parents have a hard time accepting their child. They may have unrealistically high expectations and, as a result, constantly feel that he's failing. They themselves may have received negative messages as children and may now unconsciously treat their child as they were treated.

Some parents appear to favor one of their children over another. Although it may be easy to say, "I wish you were more like your brother," or "I wish you liked science as much as your sister does," parents should recognize the harm such statements cause. Rather than motivate a child to do better, these comparisons, with their implied put-downs, make him feel badly about himself and angry. He may only be motivated to get back at the sibling who seems to enjoy more parental approval.

To see how important feedback is to self-image, consider the way you were treated as a child. If your parents valued you as a lovable, worthwhile person, you probably entered adulthood feeling good about yourself. If you received negative messages, you've probably struggled at times with a poor self-image.

What your child needs from you is acceptance, praise, and compliments on his strengths. If he never seems to please you, reconsider your expectations. They may be too high, or your parenting style may be too demanding and high-pressured. You may find that, by being more realistic, you're better able to accept your child as he is and give consistent, positive messages.

As you think about your child's self-image, you may be worried if he's shy. It's a common belief that a shy child has a negative self-image, but that's often not the case. Many children who are reserved by nature are as confident as their more outgoing peers. One teacher told a parent, "Your daughter may be quiet, but she's certainly confident when it comes to doing her work and making friends." Let your shy child know that you love him as much as you love his more extroverted siblings, and that he has as much to offer. As a result, he'll develop a healthy self-image.

A child with low self-esteem will exhibit a number of symptoms. He might struggle with friends, compete excessively with peers and siblings, misbehave, and not perform up to his ability in school.

If you're concerned about your child's self-image or have questions about the impact your attitudes have on him, talk to a parenting coach or counselor. It's much easier to resolve a child's negative feelings when he's young than it is to wait until he's older.

Am I over-scheduling my kindergarten child?

During the elementary years, children are developmentally industrious and hard working. They have plenty of energy to keep busy.

They're happy to play in unstructured ways—building forts, playing house or school, building with Legos, playing games, and playing with friends. They also enjoy the many organized activities and lessons available: sports, arts and crafts, collecting, gymnastics, dance, music, hands-on science, scouting, clubs, and more.

Many children under five or six are enrolled in too many structured programs. Toddlers and preschoolers are often too young to understand rules and lessons taught by coaches and specialists. However, as long as a kindergartner is doing what interests him and isn't feeling pressured to succeed at everything, both active play and organized programs offer kids these ages a chance to try out different experiences, find out what they like, and be with friends.

Classes, activities, and lessons (some with low or no fees required) are offered through schools, city and county recreation centers, religious organizations, individuals, and for-profit and non-profit groups. As you choose from the wealth of recreational possibilities, you should consider your child's interests, your ability to pay for classes, and the quality of individual programs. You should also ask yourself some of these questions: Will your child have friends in the class? Is practice required? Are you signing him up for your own convenience? Will the class be too rigid or too unstructured? Will a sports activity reinforce competition or teach sportsmanship? Will an art class enhance or stifle creativity? How often will the class meet? Will participating in the activity allow your child time to relax and play at home? And finally, ask yourself if you've signed him up for too many classes.

Once your kindergartner's involved in activities, if he complains about going, starts to behave in negative ways, or stops initiating a lot of play, he's probably over-scheduled. Try cutting back his participation in programs and see if it helps.

Be sure the activities your kindergartner participates in are not just ones you think he should try. Expect his interest in joining activities to increase during the elementary years. During those years, you'll know when the initiative is his, because he'll ask again and again if you've signed him up for a special program.

How do I choose the best day camp for my child?

Parents have a lot to consider before selecting a day camp for their child—cost, location, hours, transportation, the program's activities, the quality of the program, their child's interests, his friends, and the availability of after-camp day care. Since some camps fill up rapidly, parents may have to make camp decisions long before they feel ready to think about summer.

Urban and suburban areas offer many choices. There are private day camps run for profit and ones run by non-profit organizations such as the YMCA. There are municipal camps operated by cities and counties. Many private schools have summer camp programs, and some public schools are leased during the summer by private or public camps.

If you want to keep costs down, you'll find that municipal camps are the least expensive. If transportation is a problem, look for camps close to home or work, or ones offering bus transportation. If you need after-camp day care for your child, you should inquire about extended day programs.

After considering the practical side of summer arrangements, you'll still be faced with choices. Since there are general as well as specialized day camps, you should carefully consider your child's interests, skills, and personality. Would he enjoy a sports camp? Arts or music camp? Computer camp? Would he prefer an indoor camp? Would he be happier in a camp offering a mix of activities? Will he be unhappy without a friend along?

Some kids are reluctant to go to camp without knowing someone else who's going. Parents sometimes make decisions based only on where their child's friends are going. Also, some parents send all of their own children to the same camp regardless of the children's interests, because they want the siblings to be together.

As you look for camps, ask other parents for suggestions. If your child's school is the site of a summer camp, you may decide you want him to go there because it's familiar. This may be a good idea, but he may be upset if he's expecting the summer to be like the school year. He may be troubled, especially if he's only three or four years old, to see different furniture in the classrooms, different adults in charge, and different kids.

If he has special health needs, look for a camp that will make the summer pleasant and successful. For instance, one child with asthma triggered by allergens did best in an air-conditioned environment. He attended an indoor camp offering arts and crafts, sports, and computer instruction.

Your child may tell you he doesn't want to go to camp; a summer at home would be fine if your schedule can accommodate it. However, you may be put in a bind if you work or if you feel your child should be enrolled in an organized program for the summer. One solution is to look for a camp with reduced hours. You can also find out why he's reluctant to go to camp. If he doesn't want to take swimming lessons, doesn't want to take part in some of the activities, or is generally hesitant about new situations, talk to him about his feelings and offer ideas and reassurance. If necessary, seek suggestions from camp counselors or directors so that your child can have a fun camp experience. As much as possible, try to enroll your child in programs you know will be of interest to him or ones his friends will be going to. Four- and five-year-olds are often happiest going to a camp where their friends are.

Chapter 9

SCHOOL SUCCESS

- How can I choose the best child-care center or nursery school for my child?
- What should I look for when visiting a child-care center or nursery school?
- How can I feel less distant from my child's caregiver?
- Is it okay if I don't send my child to preschool?
- How should I prepare my two- to four-year-old for day care or nursery school?
- What if my child has difficulty saying good-bye when I leave him?
- Will I see changes in my child's behavior when he goes to school or day care?
- Is it normal to feel guilty or worried about sending my child to a day care center?
- When should my child learn letters and numbers?
- Why do so many children have attention deficit disorder (ADD)?
- Can day care contribute to attention deficit disorder?
- What should I do if I think my child has attention deficit disorder?
- What should I look for in recreation classes?
- How can I support my child when he's enrolled in a class?
- Should I let my child drop out of a class if he wants to?
- How do I know if my child is ready for kindergarten?
- If I'm unsure about my child's readiness for kindergarten, who can help?
- How can I encourage learning at home?
- What are the alternatives to public school?

How can I choose the best child-care center or nursery school for my child?

Every child-care center and nursery school is different, and parents have to search carefully to find a good place for their child. Schools might claim (as Montessori, Waldorf, co-op, traditional, and religious schools do) that their programs are based on familiar philosophies, but parents have to see how the philosophies are actually implemented. The personalities of staff members, the physical layout, and the day-to-day schedules are what determine a school or center's quality. The only way for parents to make an informed choice is to observe a number of programs.

There's no need to look for a preschool program that claims to prepare a child for kindergarten. The preschool years and the elementary years are different developmental stages, and if teachers and parents expect too much of a preschooler—in areas of reading, math, and writing—feelings of "I can't" and inferiority will be fostered. Learning happens gradually, and a curriculum for preschool children should not mimic what will be taught in kindergarten or first grade.

The best way to "prepare" children for the elementary years is to remember that, when they initiate play and activities, they learn to believe in themselves and learn to feel capable. This foundation is essential during the preschool years, especially because learning during the elementary years requires confidence that comes from years of initiating activities, play, exploration, and building imagination.

Parents who want a program that meets three to five mornings a week, and parents searching for a day care center open twelve hours a day will be looking for the same qualities. All parents want caring teachers and staff members, a pleasant facility, and a flexible program that will meet their child's needs for the one to four years she will attend.

The difference for parents looking at full-time day care is that their child will spend most of her waking hours at the center they choose. The selection of a quality day care program is essential.

As you look for child-care facilities, narrow your choices to centers that are easy to get to. If you're considering nursery schools, you'll probably want one close to home, while you might find a day care center more convenient if it's close to your work. Narrow your choices further by asking friends, neighbors, and co-workers for recommendations. Then visit at least two or three programs before making a decision.

What should I look for when visiting a child-care center or nursery school?

When you go to a center or school, think about the physical space. Are the rooms inviting, clean, and safe? Is there ample room to play inside, and is there play equipment outside? Are there places in the classroom where your child can play quietly? Are there a variety of toys and materials within easy reach? If it's a child-care center, where will your child take naps, and where can she go if she doesn't nap? Does the overall environment seem exciting? Does the school accept a parent's request for a particular teacher?

Watch the teachers and aides carefully, since they set the tone for the program. Do they seem to enjoy their jobs and relate well to each other? Do you like the way they interact with the children? Good teachers will be warm, understanding, and respectful of children. Do they seem reassuring and flexible enough to let a child follow her own interests? Are you comfortable with the way they set limits and carry out discipline in the classroom?

Try to imagine your child in the programs you observe. How would she react? Are the teachers' expectations appropriate for her? Would the schedule allow her flexibility? What if she wanted to continue with one activity when the teachers had scheduled a switch to another? Would she be allowed quietly to finish what she was doing?

See if the teachers pay enough attention to the children in the room. One parent saw a teacher who was so involved with a small group working on the day's curriculum project that she ignored the rest of the class. When the teacher finally became aware of an argument in the block corner, she was too late to help a child whose building had been destroyed.

Consider how many teachers there are at the center or school, and the makeup of the groups. Young children need a lot of attention and comfort. Older children need fewer adults, but the teacher-child ratio in all cases should seem satisfactory to you and meet local licensing standards. Are there mixed age groups in a single classroom, or are children placed with others the same age? You may prefer one arrangement over another.

Pay particular attention to the school or center's program. Too many are highly structured and goal-oriented, arranged with parents' and not children's needs in mind. Many teachers say, "Parents want academics. Parents expect projects." But when academics are over-emphasized, children lose opportunities to play, experiment with different materials, make discoveries, and come up with their own answers to problems. In an effective program, children have plenty of time to explore on their own, and teachers value active play and socializing—both essential for their cognitive and emotional growth.

Look at the children's artwork. Most nursery schools and centers have children do one or two art projects a day. Is the work displayed at a child's eye level? Are all the projects pre-cut by the teacher? Do all the finished projects look alike, or are they truly products of the children's effort and creativity?

Finally, see if the activities are appropriate for the children. One group of two-year-olds was expected to dye Easter eggs in school, but the children were clearly incapable of following the necessary steps. Rather than drop the activity, the teachers did all the dyeing themselves.

Teachers should build on children's interests and abilities, not give them tasks they can't perform. Look for a program that stresses exploration and discovery, and teachers who will follow up on your child's own interests and abilities. And if your child isn't enjoying school or day care, or if you think the program isn't good enough for your child, it's worth the time and effort to start your search again and switch her to a different school.

Finally, as parents try to choose the right program for their child, they often go by their gut feelings. So when you observe a preschool or child-care center, ask yourself, "Can I see my child being happy in this classroom?"

How can I feel less distant from my child's caregiver?

Ideally, parents and caregivers should relate in a cordial, informative way. However, some parents and caregivers are uncomfortable with each other and try to avoid contact.

To some parents, a caregiver may be an intimidating figure. She has influence and power over a child, and they may hesitate to alienate her with questions or complaints. They may feel that inquiries about their child will bother her, and they fear that she'll take her anger and frustration out on their child.

Some parents stay distant from a caregiver because of guilt. They feel badly about leaving their child with another adult and avoid any contact that will make them feel worse. They drop her off and pick her up as quickly as possible ("I'm so busy!") and never address the adult in charge.

There's another reason parents remain detached from their child's caregiver. They may not take her job seriously, viewing her as a babysitter and treating her as they might a neighborhood teenager. Since many caregivers are younger than the parents they work for, it may seem natural for parents to act this way.

Sometimes it's the caregiver who's reluctant to form a friendly relationship. She may feel uncomfortable with parents because she's younger and less experienced than they are. She may feel awkward telling them about their child's behavior, giving them advice, or discussing the differences between their standards and her own. She may be generally unsure of herself around adults. Many child-care workers enjoy being with children but are not as positive and confident with adults. In addition, caregivers who see parents rush in and out may hesitate to talk to them for fear of holding them up.

Here are some things you can do to improve your relationship with your child's caregiver. Take the first step, and offer a friendly hello and good-bye each day. Smile and wave if the caregiver is busy when you arrive. If she has a few minutes to chat, have a brief conversation. Talk about the weather, an upcoming weekend, the children's artwork on the wall, etc. Try to leave a few minutes at the end of the day to stay and watch your child finish a project or to talk to the other children. If you seem unhurried, the caregiver will consider you more approachable.

Caregivers want parents to pick up their child on time, let them know if there are problems at home, read school newsletters and notices, attend meetings, and comfortably discuss their child's behavior.

Most importantly, let your caregiver know you appreciate her services. She'll find it easy to talk to you about your child if she believes you take her seriously. Listen carefully to her observations and suggestions, respect her standards, be mindful of your expectations and tone, and work cooperatively with her. Be flexible when you want to make an appointment with her or when she asks to talk with you. Raise your concerns in respectful ways: "Does my child interact with other children?" "What are her strengths?" "What skills should she master?" Be polite when you ask her to make accommodations for your child. It takes time to build trust between you and those caring for your child, but effort and consistent friendliness will enhance your relationship.

Is it okay if I don't send my child to preschool?

Many parents feel pressure to send their child to nursery school since most children go to some sort of program and child-care professionals generally recommend it. Parents who keep their child home until kindergarten often face the disapproval of friends and relatives. People ask, "How will he learn to socialize?" "Isn't he ready?" "How can you get anything done with him around all day?" "Aren't you afraid he'll miss out?" "How will he be prepared for kindergarten?"

There is a number of good reasons why a child might not go to nursery school. When there's a new baby in the family, some parents keep their older child home so he won't feel rejected or pushed out. The expense of nursery school deters other families. Some parents are unable to find a nursery school they really like for their child, and some want to be with their child full time until elementary school begins. Finally, some parents keep their child at home because they welcome the freedom: when there are no school schedules to follow, parent and child can wake up when they want, go on outings together, and stay outdoors as long as they like.

A child who stays out of nursery school will not be harmed academically or socially. He'll have chances to play with siblings, neighborhood children, and friends who attend part-time or half-day programs. Parents can also enroll their child in once-a-week recreation classes and set up playdates with other children. A child can be exposed to art, music, reading, science and other activities, just as children in preschool are.

When a child does go to nursery school, his parents may marvel at how he changes. He seems more cooperative and knowledgeable, and his parents attribute this growth to the school. But parents whose children stay at home also see these changes. Young children naturally mature and develop as they get older, and a four-year-old who stays home will have the same interest in learning and playing as a four-year-old in preschool.

If your child stays home, he'll be busy and involved, especially if you provide an environment in which he can explore, play, read, go on outings, and create—all the things done at school. He'll learn about his world because, like all young children, he's curious. Nursery school can be a very positive experience, but it isn't a necessary one.

If you decide to keep your child at home for the preschool years, you may wonder how he'll adjust to kindergarten. As long as you prepare him by visiting the school ahead of time and talking about kindergarten activities, he's likely to do just as well as a child who attended preschool. Kindergarten is a new experience for all children, and they all go through a period of adjustment.

During the years that your child is at home instead of in nursery school, people will often ask him, "Where do you go to school?" and other children will tell him about their schools. Your child, particularly if he's four or five, may wonder why he isn't in school, and may feel somewhat alienated from his friends. Many children, however, are not affected by the questions and comments of others, and confidently announce, "I don't go to school," or "I learn at home." If your child does express a desire to go to nursery school, you may want to look for a program that meets your needs as well as his, or you may decide to tell him that he'll go to school when he's old enough for kindergarten.

Although the decision to keep your child home may be a difficult one, you might be surprised by unexpected support. One mother, expecting a lecture, reluctantly told her pediatrician she was not sending her child to school. The doctor shocked and delighted her by not only praising her decision, but telling her that he and his wife had kept their children home and that the experience had been very positive.

How should I prepare my two- to four-year-old for day care or nursery school?

When a child begins day care or nursery school, she and her family face the issues of separation and independence. A four-year-old will probably go without much difficulty, but many children under three have a hard time leaving their parents. Parents can make the transition from home a little easier if they talk to their child about what will be happening and patiently reassure her.

You can begin preparing a three- or four-year-old just before her new program starts. If she previously went with you to visit the school or center, remind her of what she saw. "Remember the blocks and puzzles you played with there?" If she's never seen the school, describe the building, the toys, and the activities. Let her know about snacks, lunch, and naps, and reassure her that the school has bathrooms and places for her coat and other belongings. Mention the name of someone she knows who will be in the program with her; if she doesn't know anyone in the school, tell her there will be many other children her age there. If you know who your child's teachers will be, tell her their names.

If your child is under two, you won't be able fully to prepare her for nursery school or day care, because she won't understand much of what you tell her, although you can still mention whatever you think will interest her. She'll basically have to experience the new program and the separation firsthand. You and your child's caretakers will have to be understanding and nurturing as she adjusts in the early weeks of school, and you may have to be flexible about your own schedule so you can take her home early if necessary.

On the first day of school, before you leave home, talk to your three- or four-year-old about the separation that's coming. "After we get to your classroom, I'll stay for a few minutes and then say good-bye." Tell her you'll be coming back and what your driving arrangements will be. If she'll be in a car pool, tell her who will drive. For the first few days of school you may want to do the driving yourself to help her adjust to her new situation.

What if my child has difficulty saying good-bye when I leave him?

Many children, especially those three years old and under, have a difficult time leaving their parents. Your child may want to say good-bye several times, or she may cry. Don't threaten her or say, "Be good and stop crying," or "Be a big girl." She needs support, not pressure. You might be able to eliminate some of her anxiety by letting her bring along a favorite toy or blanket. Try arriving at school fifteen minutes early so you can spend more time with her before you go. Or give her a special little treat when she gets in the car, or a "love" note or picture to carry into school with her.

You should not try to sneak out of the school without saying good-bye, even if you think such an action might keep your child from crying. Eventually she'll notice you're gone and may become frightened and upset. Although it's painful to see your child cry as you go, you should still say good-bye to her. You might feel better if you wait outside the classroom door, listening for a few minutes until she's calmed down.

As time goes by, she may continue to have trouble leaving you at the school door. Children two years old and younger don't understand that you'll return, no matter how often you tell them. This may make them anxious in the morning, and off and on throughout the day. Consult with your child's teachers. They may be able to help by giving your child extra comfort and reassurance and getting her involved in activities.

Will I see changes in my child's behavior when he goes to school or day care?

It might take your child a few weeks to adjust to school or day care, and during that time you may see some changes in behavior, such as bed-wetting, nightmares, decreased appetite, more frequent whining, and reluctance to go to school. Getting used to a program is more difficult for some children than others, but most children are affected in some way during the early days of a new situation. You'll have to be patient and understanding as your child adjusts.

If, after several weeks, she's still showing behavioral changes and seems unhappy, talk to her teachers, and stay to observe the program. You might even drop in unexpectedly to see how she is and to try to find out why she isn't enjoying herself. As you watch her, ask yourself the following questions: Does she seem to have friends she enjoys? Is she one of the youngest children in the group? (If she is, she may feel less confident and accepted.) Is she getting enough attention from her teachers? If the program seems inappropriate, take her out and find a better one. But if you're unsure, wait a bit before making your decision. Your child just might need an extra amount of understanding and time to adjust to day care or school.

Is it normal to feel guilty or worried about sending my child to a day care center?

When parents work full time outside the home, they often send their child to a day care center. Yet eight to twelve hours a day, five days a week, is a long time for parents and children to be apart, and the separation can take an emotional toll on parents. They miss their child, particularly when he first begins a program, and worry about the care he's receiving. Is he happy? Safe? Are his teachers taking an interest in him? Does he have friends?

Parents may feel guilty because they fear that day care will have a negative effect on their child. If they see his behavior change, they wonder if it's because of his program. They may feel bad about not spending enough time with him, and a mother, especially, may wonder whether she should have gone to work full time in the first place. Even when parents and child are together in the evenings, the effects of work and day care continue. There's never enough time together at home, and parents who want time for themselves may feel guilty about not paying enough attention to their child.

If you're concerned about having your child in a full-time program, your feelings are natural. There are things you can do to lessen your guilt and worry, and to solve some of the child-care–related problems you experience. The most important step is to reassure yourself about your child's well-being by staying in close contact with his teachers. Call the center periodically, and find out how he's doing. If the teachers agree (and they should), ask that he be brought to the phone so you can talk to him. When you have a chance, drop by the day care center unannounced so you can observe him at play. You'll feel better if you see him happily involved.

If you suspect that he's not happy, don't ignore the problem, even if you feel desperate about the need for child care. It takes a great deal of effort and energy to become involved in your child's day care situation; some parents avoid or deny all problems because they don't have the time, desire, or energy to cope. Others are afraid even to question their child about his day for fear he'll say something negative.

If you're worried about your child's adjustment to day care, you have to become involved enough to help him. Make sure the quality of his program remains high—don't compromise. Spend as much time as possible with him—playing and doing activities together—when you're home in the evenings and on weekends. Look to other parents for support and advice. Don't leave him at day care when you have a day off work. Instead, take him with you to run errands. And finally, reconsider your need to work outside the home or to work full time. You and your child could benefit greatly if you were able to stay home with him as much as possible during the few short years before elementary school.

When should my child learn letters and numbers?

Many preschool and day care programs claim to be "academic," teaching very young children to count, recite the alphabet, and learn various concepts. Such emphasis on educational activities is part of a larger, society-wide push to have children learn more, faster. Publishers put out educational books and software; toy companies manufacture educational games; television shows teach the alphabet and numbers. Because of pressure from friends, neighbors, some child development professionals, and the media, many parents feel concerned if their young child hasn't yet learned shapes, colors, letters, and numbers.

It's possible to teach a young child to memorize and then recite back almost any short list, including the numbers from one to ten and the alphabet. A three-year-old may know that saying "One, two, three, four," is called counting, but she probably won't understand that the number eight represents eight objects until she's four or five.

A child can't be taught to understand concepts before she's developmentally ready. Gradually, as she's read to and as she experiments, plays with objects, asks questions, observes her environment, and explores, she'll learn what words and numbers mean. If her natural curiosity is encouraged and she has materials to experiment with, she'll learn concepts easily. But too much emphasis on early education may discourage a child and diminish her natural drive to learn. Parents can wait until their child shows a spontaneous interest in letters, words, and concepts, and then follow up on what she can do.

There's no need for schools and parents to provide excessive amounts of educational materials for young children. Colors, shapes, numbers, and words are part of whatever children do, so they learn about these things naturally. Every day, a child hears, "You're wearing blue shorts," "Do you want the red or the green crayon?" "Here are three crackers," or "Look at that big truck." Parents talk about rainy days and sunny days; names of birds, animals, and flowers; the different seasons; and more. A child has constant exposure to such concepts as same and different (milk is different than juice; Mom is different than Dad), soft and hard, big and little. She hears adults counting, sees them reading, and observes letters and numbers everywhere. She gets a natural jump on literacy when her parents read to her daily, patiently repeating her favorite stories.

You'll hear your child ask, "How many is this?" "What color is this?" "What does this say?" "What's that?" She'll begin to count out loud, at first getting the numbers out of order, and she'll write letters on paper, often creating nonsense words, or writing letters or her name backwards. Try not to correct her, but rather encourage her to keep counting and keep writing. She'll learn at her own pace—

without pressure—because young children are interested and self-motivated. Then starting with kindergarten and first grade, you'll see her make great strides in literacy and math. And if you consistently show an interest in learning and discovery, encourage your child, and nurture her interests, she'll follow your lead and always find excitement and joy in learning.

Why do so many children have attention deficit disorder (ADD)?

ADD has become a common—and at times controversial—childhood "disorder." Children are diagnosed with it when they have trouble paying attention to tasks, especially ones they're not interested in. While a preschooler may be identified as having ADD, more often a child is diagnosed during the early elementary years, when teachers or parents begin complaining about how distractible a child is. "He just doesn't focus." "He doesn't sit still or follow directions."

There's no consistent chemical evidence for ADD, and while it's certainly a real disorder, a growing number of people feel that it's over-diagnosed by pediatricians, therapists, and even educators. Children who truly have ADD typically have additional neuro-biological difficulties including visual, auditory, or motor problems. But any child who says, "I forgot," and who dawdles before going to school; procrastinates when getting dressed, doing homework, or doing chores; is boisterous, aggressive, or temperamental; or gets involved in something other than what he's directed to do, could potentially be labeled ADD and medicated for the condition.

One mother gave two examples of what she believed was ADD-like behavior in her four-year-old. "He sits at dinner with one leg hanging off the side of the chair, and he doesn't listen when I tell him to stay close by me in the mall." When asked what she does about these things, she responded, "Nothing! He has ADD, so he can't help it."

Too often, the diagnosis of ADD and the medication that follows are either a catch-all method of dealing with a seemingly difficult, but normal, child or an excuse for not setting firm limits, spending time with him, and meeting his needs at home or at school. Parents and teachers worried by the increase in ADD diagnoses need to know that there are a variety of other, more common reasons why a young child would have trouble listening to adults or paying attention to his responsibilities.

Many children are simply spirited by nature, or they may act out in aggressive ways because they're not receiving enough calm, positive attention. A child may feel stress because of his parents' divorce, a new sibling, tension, and yelling at home, or school pressures. Often, parents haven't helped their child learn to get along with others, and haven't given him enough limits, guidance, and discipline. Other aspects to consider are the quick-paced lifestyle children are expected to live, the constant exposure to TV and video games, and the click of the computer mouse taking children from one busy site to another.

Can day care contribute to attention deficit disorder?

A rarely discussed contributor to ADD-like behavior can be day care, where many children, starting at age two, follow a rigid schedule initiated by teachers. Frequent changes from one activity to another mean a child can't focus for long periods or get involved in something interesting without constant interruptions. The schedule basically trains him not to pay careful attention.

Here's a typical day for a young child in a day care program. He may wake as early as 5:30 a.m. so his family can leave home by 6:00 to get to day care by 6:30. He's rushed as he gets dressed, and there's no time to play before driving off. Once he arrives at the center, his schedule is packed (only naptime lasts longer than an hour).

6:30	Arrives and says goodbye to his parents, whom he won't see again for ten to twelve hours
6:30–7:00	Breakfast
7:00–8:00	Table games, puzzles, quiet activities
8:00–8:30	Story
8:30–9:15	Art activity
9:15–9:45	Snack
9:45–10:30	Outdoor play (with a lot of time spent sharing equipment: "You have five minutes to ride the bike, and then it's Ben's turn.")
10:30–11:15	Circle time (teacher directed lessons)
11:15–11:30	Song and movement activity
11:30–12:00	Lunch
12:00–2:00	Nap
2:00–2:30	Snack
2:30–3:15	Outdoor play
3:15–4:00	Free play (coloring, play dough, cutting, and block building)
4:00–4:30	Learning centers (reading, weather, holidays, and science)
4:30–5:00	Music
5:00–6:00	Table activities, puzzles, cleanup, and preparation to leave.

At 6:00 p.m., the child is picked up and taken home or on an errand. His family arrives home between 6:30 and 7:00, and he plays or watches TV until dinner from 7:00 to 7:30. Then he plays for a short while before bath, story, and bed at 8:30, or later if he had a long nap at school.

Children do this day after day, often for three, four, or five years. While the day care schedule may seem to keep them busy and enriched, it actually operates counter to their needs. According to developmentalist Erik Erikson, preschoolers have important tasks at this developmental stage: they need a lot of time to initiate ideas; plan, discover, carry out, and persevere in activities; and set goals. This is how children learn to focus, concentrate, and follow through.

Yet children in many day care programs are not focusing and following through enough. All day, they're required to stop, share, or give up whatever they're using before they're done. They often don't have time to finish what they start before teachers interrupt to get them ready for the next activity. The constant starting and stopping and the lack of flexibility keep children from learning to concentrate for extended periods—a necessary function of the developing brain. The frustration of not being able to finish what they start or having to share before they've finished using something can make children uncooperative and fidgety. By the time a child gets to kindergarten or first grade, his teachers may be pointing out his ADD-like behavior.

What should I do if I think my child has attention deficit disorder?

If you suspect your child has ADD, or if he's already been diagnosed, don't give him medication unless you and your physician believe it's absolutely necessary. There are many other strategies you can try first. If he's in day care, look for programs with more flexible schedules. Limit TV, video games, and computer time; instead spend more time with him, playing together and paying attention to his interests. Highlight his capabilities, nurture his curiosity, and give him opportunities to initiate activities. Slow down, let him finish what he starts, and don't stress cleanup over discovery and creativity.

You also need to make discipline a priority. Set clear limits on his inappropriate behavior, follow through with consequences, and redirect him toward positive activities. Look for underlying reasons for his misbehavior. Help him learn to control his impulses, and consistently teach him right from wrong.

All children have some trouble concentrating and need prompting and reminders, especially when they'd rather be doing something else. If your child shows ADD-like behavior, it will take time for him to learn to focus on important tasks. But with your involvement and patience and his teachers' cooperation, he should eventually be able to follow directions and pay attention—without needing medication.

What should I look for in recreation classes?

Parents enroll their child in recreation classes so he can pick up new skills and enjoy himself. Sometimes these classes are well-run and satisfying, but other times they're poorly taught and disappointing. In order to choose classes wisely, try to observe programs before registering, and consider which activities are most appropriate. Then, once class sessions begin, monitor the program, and help your child adjust.

Before you sign up for a class, watch a session taught by the instructor your child will have. Although it may be difficult for you to arrange an observation, it's worth the effort. Many programs and classes sound exciting when described in catalogs and brochures, but turn out to be boring or inadequate. If possible, take your child along so he can let you know if he's interested.

As you watch a class session, ask yourself these questions: How structured is the program? Does it look like fun? Do the children seem to be enjoying themselves? How does the instructor respond to a child who's hesitant about joining the group? Is there unnecessary pressure on children to conform and achieve? Does the teacher seem to nurture creativity? Does she say, "I like the way you did that," rather than, "You can do better than that"? Does she accept a child's limitations? How large is the class? Do children get a chance to show the teacher what they can do? Do they have to spend much time waiting for turns?

How can I support my child when he's enrolled in a class?

Briefly prepare him for the first session. Talk to him about the instructors, the equipment, the clothes he'll wear, and any friends who'll be in the class. Let him know about transportation arrangements and where you'll be sitting while the class meets. And since most children wonder about the availability of bathrooms, tell him that the program has bathrooms.

On the first day of class, you'll notice that some children quickly join in the activities, while others have difficulty adjusting. If your child is reluctant to get involved, you might feel discouraged and embarrassed, especially if the other class members are having an easy time. You might also feel alone, questioning your parenting abilities and wondering what you've done to make your child shy and unwilling to participate. You might also feel angry at your child, particularly if it was his idea to take the class.

In such a situation, a supportive teacher, coach, or instructor can help by smiling, waving, coming over to talk, and generally letting your child know he's accepted even if he doesn't choose to participate right away. You'll also feel more comfortable if the other parents in the group are supportive rather than judgmental. While you're encouraging your child to participate, try not to pressure him, but rather accept his hesitancy, and, if necessary, sit with him until he's ready to join the group.

In later class sessions, he may continue to resist joining in or may become disenchanted with the program. Perhaps the instructor overwhelms him, the other children seem too big, he's not ready to separate from you, the teachers' (or your) expectations create too much pressure, he's unwilling to join in because you're watching, or the class is not what he thought it would be. He may have had his own fantasies about the program, imagining he'd be free to jump on the trampoline, do somersaults, or improvise his own craft projects. But most programs allow little freedom—children are told what to do and how to do it, and they spend a lot of time waiting for their turns.

Should I let my child drop out of a class if he wants to?

It's not unusual for a child's interest in a recreation program to dwindle as the weeks go by. You may hear, "I'll go another day," or "I don't want to go." Often because of a rigid structure or competition, the classes stop being fun. Think back to your own experience with recreation programs. The classes that you enjoyed and continued to attend were ones that provided fun, acceptance, and positive feedback. The ones you disliked made you feel unaccepted and pressured.

If your child wants to drop out of a recreation class, discuss the situation with him and then with the instructors. They can help you decide whether you should spend some sessions helping your child adjust or whether he should stop attending. Don't force him to continue in a class he's not enjoying, since such pressure is likely to increase his resistance to taking other classes. And don't worry that quitting will make him a habitual "quitter." He's too young to have understood what he was getting into or to need a lesson in perseverance. Just continue to expose him to a variety of experiences and activities so he can figure out what interests him and develop new skills.

How do I know if my child is ready for kindergarten?

As your child approaches the end of his preschool years, you'll probably begin to consider his readiness for kindergarten. Some parents confidently envision their child in kindergarten, but others, particularly those whose children have mid- to late-in-the-year birthdays (based on the school's cut-off date), wonder if he's ready for this major step. Most school districts let parents choose whether to enroll their child during his fifth or sixth year. Because a child's success in the first year of school lays the foundation for later success, the decision to send a child to kindergarten must be made carefully and in his best interests.

Parents sometimes assume that a child who's been to day care or nursery school is automatically prepared for kindergarten, but it's a different experience in a number of ways. Children in kindergarten are expected to spend scheduled amounts of time sitting and working on specific academic skills. Although play is considered part of the daily program, emphasis is placed on group and individual academic work, and on following a set curriculum. Kindergartners become part of a large school community that operates under new rules and expectations. And children find that their parents, who are excited about kindergarten, may begin to put emphasis on "doing well."

Chronological age is the major factor determining kindergarten readiness, but there naturally are related factors parents should consider: cognitive or intellectual development, social and emotional development, and physical size. If your child is five to eleven months younger than other kindergartners, he may display behavior that's significantly different from his classmates'. Even if he's advanced in one area of development, such as academics, he may generally be functioning at a level lower than expected for his age group.

To evaluate overall readiness for kindergarten, parents should first look at their child's cognitive development. When a child is functioning academically below kindergarten level, he can sometimes be helped through individualized instruction from teachers and specialists. But the child who's lagging behind often has a hard time catching up, because learning in certain areas may be difficult for him. Despite the instructional support, he might think he's "not as good" as his peers, and he may feel unnecessary stress because he can't cope with the demands of school. When this happens, he'll probably show signs of disliking school, say he hates school, or exhibit behavioral problems. Academic struggles in kindergarten often establish a pattern that can continue for years.

Another area of concern should be social and emotional development. A child who's socially or emotionally immature may have a difficult time adjusting to his teacher's demands. He may seem unwilling to behave as kindergartners should, when actually he's unable to act more mature. He may have a hard time working and playing cooperatively with his classmates, and this may cause him to be labeled a "behavior problem." Naturally, if he's labeled this way, his self-image will be affected, and ultimately, he may continue misbehaving because he feels frustrated and angry over his inability to do what's expected of him.

A child who lags behind socially but is advanced academically poses a dilemma for his parents, who may be concerned about holding him back an extra year. They may think he will not be challenged in academic areas if he waits and attends kindergarten with younger children, yet, if the imbalance between social and intellectual development is striking, he's probably not developmentally ready for kindergarten.

Another factor parents should consider is size and physical development. When a child is several months younger than the average kindergarten student, he may also be smaller than his classmates. Size and age are important to young children, who frequently check each other to see who's tallest or oldest. And since children often begin to lose their teeth during the kindergarten year, a younger child might be frustrated and unhappy if he doesn't lose teeth when his older friends do. Being the youngest and smallest can put a child in a vulnerable position in the classroom, although this would naturally be more of a problem for a child who's reserved and quiet rather than boisterous and outgoing.

If I'm unsure about my child's readiness for kindergarten, who can help?

Other adults who know your child, including professionals, can help. If your child has been to day care or nursery school, the first people you contact will probably be his teachers. Since they have a basic understanding of kindergarten requirements and have had many opportunities to observe children, they'll be able to advise you. As long as you like and trust them, their judgment may be very helpful. If you continue to have questions, seek the opinion of a developmental specialist who assesses school readiness. Your pediatrician may also be of help in addressing your concerns. Friends who have held their children back a year can share their thoughts with you, and elementary school counselors or principals will discuss the issue and offer information on kindergarten readiness. You might also want to visit a kindergarten classroom and ask yourself if you can picture your child there, ready for formal schooling.

Most parents who have held their children back a year have not regretted taking the extra time for growing and maturing. And most preschool programs offer pre-kindergarten classes. A child who starts kindergarten when he's developmentally ready is better able to meet academic demands and get along with others throughout his schooling. When children don't have to struggle to keep up—academically, socially, or emotionally—they develop a strong sense of self-confidence, and this provides a good founda-tion for the school years.

How can I encourage learning at home?

Learning is not just something that happens at school, and learning is not dependent on formal lessons. A family that is involved, inter-ested, and curious can learn all the time.

The best way parents can encourage learning at home is to be learners themselves. When parents read, kids read. When parents have many interests, kids develop interests and hobbies too. Parents show positive attitudes toward learning whenever they try to master a skill, research a new topic, or spend time at a museum or concert.

An important way you can enrich your child's education is to follow up on your child's interests by providing materials, books, and experiences. With imagination and a creative use of available resources, even parents on the most limited budgets can offer active encouragement.

For example, if your child's interested in rocks, look for colorful picture guides in the library or on the Internet, or visit collections in local museums and nature centers. Take him to local gem and mineral shows. In addition, he can collect and organize pictures of rocks and minerals from magazines and advertisements, and arrange his collection in a homemade display case. There's no limit to the ways you can follow up on your child's interests. Help him find activities that meet his needs, and allow him to explore a hobby or skill as fully as he desires.

If your child wants to pursue an academic subject, encourage him to go beyond the school's lessons. A child who likes the chal-lenge of math can be introduced to puzzles, chess, or new computer software. There are many math games, puzzles, and curiosities for children available in libraries, bookstores, and on the Internet. All will stimulate a child more than the "educational workbooks" often marketed to parents.

As your child grows, you can also help by talking regularly to him about his schoolwork, his interests, and current events. Discussions can revolve around sports, the environment, history, popular entertainment, space exploration, fashion, music, or animals. As long as the subject is interesting to your child, the talk will be valuable. Listen carefully to his opinions and questions. That way, he'll come to see himself as an important part of family talks.

Learning doesn't have to be parent-initiated. A child can teach his parents and siblings a new skill or share a new fact, and he can learn from his siblings. To enrich your child's education at home, tell stories, encourage him to tell you stories, make regular trips to the library, get your child his own subscription to a children's magazine, and leave a child's dictionary and encyclopedia out. Increase your child's vocabulary by using new words. Go to the zoo, museums, nature centers, concerts, events, and children's plays together. Watch educational programs, particularly ones on nature.

Make learning a pleasurable, shared experience, and your child will join in. Don't give negative judgments about his progress or compare his achievements to his siblings'. He'll do better without pressure, including the stress of being over-programmed.

Finally, a fun, loving, and nurturing home will help your child develop a life-long love of learning.

What are the alternatives to public school?

Many parents are dissatisfied with their child's public school education. They know their child's potential, and they've seen her enthusiasm and capacity for learning. Yet in public school she may be consistently unhappy, bored, or unchallenged. Parents who feel that their local public school isn't benefiting their child can consider transferring her to a better public school, or a public magnet or charter school. If these choices are unavailable or unsatisfactory, parents can look at other alternatives.

The most common are private schools. Many parents don't consider private education because of the costs. Yet some private schools are less expensive than others, many offer scholarships, some are co-ops accepting volunteer work in place of tuition, some help arrange loans, and some offer free or reduced tuition for parents who are employed by the school. When considering costs, you should evaluate your priorities. Some parents decide to invest in their child's education, and accept a simpler and less costly lifestyle in exchange.

Some parents are wary of private school for another reason. They fear their child will lose the social benefits of attending a neighborhood school. While most private schools encourage a strong sense of community and plan many social activities for their students, it is true that a child who doesn't attend his neighborhood school will probably have a smaller social circle. However, private school students can still play with their neighborhood friends after school and on weekends in organized activities and on sports teams.

Parents who choose private education do so because they want a social, moral, academic, or religious atmosphere they can't find in public schools. Some parents have always known—either because of their own backgrounds or because they have firm preferences for a particular type of education—that they would send their child to private school. More often, they choose private school because they're unhappy with their child's public school. They may want their child to experience smaller classes, less emphasis on preparing for standardized tests, and a more challenging curriculum. While some parents plan on a full thirteen years of private education, some only want private school for the early elementary years. However, many parents find it hard to put a child back into public school, since they often find private school more effective and individualized.

There are many kinds of private schools: religious, Montessori, Waldorf, college preparatory, academically accelerated, and schools for children with learning disabilities or emotional problems. In large urban areas there are many choices, while small cities or rural areas may have fewer options.

Parents who don't know what they want should begin by visiting private schools. They can talk to each school's principal or admissions counselor, attend an open house, and sit in on a class. When observing a school, look for answers to these questions: What are kids expected to achieve? How does the teacher present material? How does she relate to the class? Is there an assistant in the class? How structured is the work and classroom atmosphere? Do the students seem happy and interested? Would your child's learning style and personality be a match here?

Parents should ask other families for advice about private schools and, if necessary, consult an educational specialist who can test and observe a child, interview parents, and then recommend likely schools.

For parents who choose not to look at private schools but are unhappy with the public ones, there's another alternative—home schooling. A growing number of families have children who learn at home, taught by their parents. Many local school districts allow home education, and some districts cooperate with home schoolers, letting them use school resources.

People are often shocked when they first hear of home schooling. "How can parents teach their child?" "How will she learn to get along with other kids?"

The fact is, most parents who are able to make the significant time commitment can successfully teach their child. Kids in school spend much of each day marking time. They wait in line, wait for their turn to read, wait to have their questions answered. They do "busy work" while the teacher works with other students. They sit while she disciplines others. Very little of the typical school day is actually spent learning. When a child is schooled at home, she can master material quickly and efficiently.

Home-schooled children usually get along fine socially. Like private-school children, they still play with neighborhood friends and join them in organized activities such as classes, teams, and scouts. They don't miss out on much socializing at school, because socializing is generally discouraged at school. Students are rewarded for being quiet and reprimanded for talking to friends during class. During recess, interaction may be competitive, fueled by students' need to be smarter, better, faster than classmates. A child learning at home doesn't get caught up in that competition and for that reason may get along better with other children.

Since you're familiar with your child's learning style and interests, you can individualize her work. Sometimes you can use books; other times you can do hands-on projects with her. Her schooling can also include frequent trips to museums, libraries, performances, and nature centers. Many home schoolers give their children standardized tests once a year to be sure they're making good progress. Find out what tests your school district gives, and either ask to have your child tested with other students or ask for a copy of the test to administer at home.

If you're considering home schooling, explore the many resources available. There are supportive national and local home-schooling organizations. There are also curriculum guides available from school systems, local libraries, the Internet, and educational bookstores. You might decide to follow the plan offered by a correspondence school or get together with other home schoolers to share material.

One of the hardest parts of picking an alternative to public school, whether private or home schooling, is dealing with the criticism of other adults. Families who are satisfied with public school may be intolerant of your choices. "I think it's crazy to keep your child out of school!" "Why spend all that money for private school? It's so unnecessary!" They may also feel threatened because you've chosen a path different from their own.

It's unpleasant to be judged. But the unpleasantness is more than made up for by the satisfaction of seeing your child blossom in a new school environment. Because of the choices you've made, your child may flourish in ways she never would have otherwise.

Chapter 10

TOUGH QUESTIONS

- How will divorce affect my young child?
- Is there a way to make my divorce easier on my child?
- How can we adjust to our blended family?
- How do I respond to my child's questions about death?
- How can I encourage self-confidence?
- What can I do about lying?

How will divorce affect my young child?

Parents in the midst of separation or divorce can easily feel over-whelmed. They must deal with their own emotional, legal, and financial problems, and often have little energy left for their children. Yet children suffer greatly during a divorce and need special attention just at a time when parents are least able to give it.

When parents are caught up in a divorce, they often don't see their child's distress clearly. They may feel helpless and guilty and, as a result, deny his needs. "He'll be fine." "The kids will keep busy." "Their father worked such long hours, he didn't spend much time with them anyway." "He wasn't such a good father. They'll hardly miss him."

Young children don't ask directly for help or reassurance. Instead, they act sad, angry, and frustrated. Siblings will fight, cry, and whine more, or may misbehave in school. Children (typically under three) who act as though everything's fine are simply too young to under-stand what a divorce means, and so it may take time before they show their anxious feelings. They have to go through the experience to begin their understanding of it.

Divorce can cause lifelong strain for children. They can grow up to distrust relationships and fear being hurt. The roots of such emotional damage lie in the way children think about and experi-ence divorce.

Four- and five-year-olds may blame themselves for the separa-tion. They know that parents sometimes argue about child-rearing, and they can feel responsible for their parents' fights, thinking they should have been good or listened more. "If only I'd listened more." Children also believe that their wishes are very powerful. Since they've sometimes had negative thoughts about their parents, they can believe those thoughts caused the divorce.

Related to this is a child's intense desire to have his parents back together. Even when the relationship was tense and argumentative, a young child will want his parents to stay together. And much as parents may want their child's approval of the divorce, a young child won't believe that living apart is best. Instead, he'll talk, dream, and wish for a reconciliation, and when one doesn't come, he might feel angry at himself for his powerlessness and angry at his parents for ignoring his desires: "I want Daddy to live here."

Both parents have to deal with these feelings. There should be respectful communication between them and their children, and a sense that sad and angry thoughts are acceptable. Kids should talk, and parents should listen and reflect back what they've heard. "I know you feel sad." After a child has expressed his feelings, parents have to continually reassure him. "It's not your fault Daddy and I don't live together anymore."

Children need to ask lots of questions, and parents should listen and respond, even when it's very difficult. "Where will Daddy live? Will we see him? Why can't he sleep here? Will he ever live here again?" "If Mommy was the only woman in the world, would you marry her again?"

If a child learns that his parents have stopped loving each other, he'll worry at times that they'll stop loving him, too. He needs to know by words and actions that both parents love him very much, and that, no matter how angry the parent he lives with is, he or she will never leave him. He'll also want to know he can still see his grandparents and other relatives who've been close to him.

Is there a way to make my divorce easier on my child?

It's very important (now and throughout his childhood) for your child to have regular, frequent communication and visits with the parent not living at home. A child loves both parents and will have an easier time adjusting if he spends time with the one not living with him often. Parents must always reject the impulse to belittle each other or try to get their child to take sides. Although this can be very difficult if the divorce was bitter, parents must keep their child's needs and feelings in mind. If a child is put in the middle of an emotional tug-of-war, he'll feel pressured, guilty, and disloyal.

As you help your child, offer him outlets for his feelings and try to smooth the way as much as possible. Talk to his teacher, and ask for her support. Read about how divorce impacts children. Learn what divorce is like through the eyes of a child. You can try reading your child a book about children dealing with divorce, but young children aren't easily comforted by others' experiences or feelings; they're still too egocentric. You can write a story, using your child's words, about his feelings. Even when you're emotionally drained, stretch yourself, and offer comfort when he cries or needs extra hugs and attention.

Since you'll be busy and carrying a bigger workload without your spouse, you might be tempted to put some of the burden on your older child. The period during and immediately after a divorce is not the time to give him additional responsibilities. He might especially resent doing jobs his now-absent parent did.

Whatever you do to try and ease your child's way, understand that you can't fully keep him from suffering because of your divorce. Take his emotional responses seriously, and consider contacting a counselor or divorce coach for support and guidance. It is often true that children who grow up in divorced families are more vulnerable and have a greater risk of a variety of problems involving school performance, self-esteem, and getting along with others.

Parents don't want the breakup of their marriage to harm their child. Before divorce, many parents seek advice about minimizing their child's suffering. During and after the divorce, most parents' love and concern for their child remain unchanged. Yet, the stress of divorce can be so intense that parents eventually find it hard to keep concentrating on their child's needs.

Divorce is almost always devastating for kids. Many parents want to believe their child will bounce back: "Kids are so resilient." "He'll get over it after a little while." But children don't recover easily. Some may seem unaffected simply because they have busy schedules and many distractions. Others keep their feelings to themselves for fear of further upsetting or angering their parents. A child who's confused, ashamed, or embarrassed may hide or deny his feelings rather than talk about this tough issue. And many emotions are repressed.

What a child of divorce feels is sadness, anger, hurt, and sometimes a sense of abandonment. Even if he was exposed to frequent turmoil when his parents were together, he usually won't greet the divorce with relief. Almost all kids want their families to stay together, and they feel powerless when they can't make their wish come true. One five-year-old whose parents had been separated for a year told her friend, "For my birthday I don't want any presents. I just want my family to have dinner together again." These are big burdens for any child who finds the condition of his family life and the state of his childhood dramatically changed.

Even the most comfortable parts of a child's life may suddenly become stressful after divorce. Dinner and bedtime may be awkward. Family celebrations may be uncomfortable, and relationships with grandparents, aunts, uncles, and cousins may be strained or even cut off.

If parents are very angry about the divorce, all aspects of a child's everyday life will be affected. Some parents may coerce their child into taking sides, leaving him feeling uncomfortable.

All these potentially negative experiences and feelings, if not dealt with carefully by parents, can cause great emotional harm. A child may develop a poor self-image, distrust, a pessimistic outlook, or depression. He also may have trouble in school or with peers and siblings.

During and following a divorce, parents have to commit themselves to putting their child's needs first—to consistently giving love and attention, and being deeply involved in his life. He needs extra affection and understanding during and after a breakup, and he needs both of his parents to be nurturers and role models.

To help, parents must refrain from speaking ill of each other in their child's presence. The parent who does not live with the child has to have frequent contact, drive carpools, go to his special events, and help with schoolwork. If a parent does not stay involved, the child will feel rejected and unworthy of love.

If the practical side of parenting seems overwhelming, simplify your life to make more time for your child. Have easy meals, let some housekeeping chores go, or cut back on outside commitments.

Over time your child may begin to understand and accept his situation, although the experience of divorce will be difficult for years, perhaps for the rest of his life. Most children grow up wishing there had never been a divorce and greet their adult years with a desire (and commitment) not to put their own children through a divorce.

While some divorces are necessary, many children endure too much stress and anxiety as a result of their parents not working out their differences. Divorce is a decision that needs to be made very, very carefully—and yes, with children in mind.

How can we adjust to our blended family?

All families have to work at living in harmony. Blended families have to try particularly hard. Stepparents rarely feel the same bond with a stepchild that they do with their natural children. Adjusting to life in a blended family requires much commitment, patience, and understanding.

Parents may have an easier time if they understand their child's point of view. Because he's still adjusting to his parents' divorce, he may fear attachment to another adult who might leave. He also may worry about losing the love and attention of his newly married parent, seeing the stepparent as an intruder and rival.

When a stepparent joins a family, many rituals and routines change, and a young child can find this upsetting and confusing. The stepparent is another authority figure, and a young child will react to new or different rules and restrictions. "Why do I have to go to bed now? You're not my mom."

A child who resents a stepparent may act on his feelings in a number of ways. He may be intentionally uncooperative and belligerent, fantasizing that his actions will bring his natural parents together again.

He may use his stepparent as a target for his frustration and anger: "It's never fun going to dinner anymore because of Ellen."

Another complication in blended families is the presence of stepsiblings. In a blended family, kids are thrown together with new siblings and forced to play, share possessions and perhaps even a bedroom, and compete for attention from parents. It's natural that stepsiblings get upset over perceived unfairness. And if the parents in a remarriage have different discipline standards, stepsiblings will argue about who has to listen to which adult.

In spite of the difficulties, blended families can succeed. To help your family during its adjustment, look for stepfamily support groups in your area. They offer an opportunity to talk about concerns, hear tips on getting along, and listen to other families' experiences. You also might consider using a therapist to help improve your family's relationships.

If you're a stepparent, be patient as you get to know your stepchild. Take an interest in his activities. Don't create or enforce rules unless you have a good relationship with him, and don't try to replace his absent natural parent. If he rejects you, look for possible openings. Will he let you help with a puzzle? Play a game? Can you play ball, cook, plant a garden, sing, or read together?

If you're the natural parent, spend time alone with your child, reinforcing your relationship. Praise him if he tries to get along with his stepfamily: "I know it's hard sometimes." Remind your child often that disrespectful behavior is not acceptable. Take on the role of disciplinarian for him, rather than leaving that responsibility to your new spouse.

Be sensitive to the difficulty stepsiblings have with their arrangements. It takes time for kids to adjust to each other. As they get older, sometimes ask them for suggestions about getting along and dealing with conflicts.

As you adjust to your blended family, it's important that your marriage remain loving and stable. Remarriages are often difficult, and stepfamily tension coupled with everyday stress can be very disruptive. If you put time and effort into your relationship with your spouse, you'll not only strengthen the bonds of your marriage, but your bonds with your child as well. When he sees that you love and enjoy each other, he'll gradually learn to accept his situation.

How do I respond to my child's questions about death?

All young children have some experience with death. They may have lost a pet, seen a dead bird or squirrel, watched TV coverage of war or a tragic accident, or overheard their parents talking about death. They also hear about death and dying in fairy tales and movies. Developmentally, preschoolers can't understand the permanence of death.

Whatever the circumstances, talking to a child about death is difficult, especially if you're grieving. You may feel overwhelmed by your own sadness and unable to meet your child's needs. In addition, speaking about death forces parents to confront their own questions and fears, and reminds them of their mortality.

Even when parents aren't mourning a personal loss, a child's questions can make parents uncomfortable. "Why did he die?" "Will our cat wake up?" "Why couldn't the doctor make him better?" "What happens to people after they die?" Although there are no easy answers, when explaining death to a three- to five-year-old, try putting it in terms they can understand, "When people die, they don't move anymore." "When dogs die, they don't bark anymore."

If your family has experienced a loss, the most important thing you can do is talk to your child and comfort her. Find out what she thinks and, if necessary, correct her misconceptions and reassure her. Let her share her feelings. She may also want to talk about her fears that you or she will die. "I think you will live a long time." She may also tell you, "I'm not going to die!" There's no need to correct her if she says this. Use the opportunity to just listen. Her understanding of death will change as she gets a little older.

Some children don't talk at all about their loss. If your child shows no sign of mourning, or if she seems to be coping too well, either she's too young to express her feelings, or she may be holding her feelings in. If she's four or five, you can probably talk to her about the person who died and help her express her sadness so her feelings don't become overwhelming. Let her know that although the person she loved has died, his or her love will never go away.

It's often difficult to know if a young child should attend the funeral of someone she was close to. This is a decision family members must make depending on their culture, religious practices, and beliefs. Other considerations are the relationship a child had with the person and the child's age. It's sometimes better for a child to be with her parents than to feel excluded or frightened at home. If you take your child to a funeral, explain (to your four- or five-year-old) what the funeral will be like. Let her know that people will be sad. "Aunt Jan is crying because she's sad that Uncle Alex died."

If she doesn't want to go, respect her decision. One five-year-old told her parents, "I don't like funerals, and whenever you ask me if I want to go to one the answer is NO."

As she struggles with her feelings, remember that the feeling of loss can last for weeks, months, or even years, depending on how close she was to the person who died. With time and help from you and others, your child will gradually come to terms with her loss.

How can I encourage self-confidence?

One of the most important tasks you have is to consistently let your child know she's capable, loved, and worthy of attention. Her self-esteem is based largely on feedback you give her. If you show you value her, she'll generally feel good about herself. If you concentrate on her faults and don't encourage her, she may develop a poor self-image.

Some parents are not supportive. In an effort to improve their child's behavior or to express frustration and disappointment, they speak harshly. "You're not a good listener." "Stop acting like a baby." "What's wrong with you?" "You know better!" "You're not nice." A child who hears these messages learns that she can't easily please her parents or live up to their standards.

She gradually starts to believe that her skills, abilities, personality, or appearance aren't good enough. In such circumstances, it's hard for a child to develop confidence.

Some parents who speak negatively to their child were themselves criticized as children and may have grown up with a lack of confidence. Even though they once struggled against harsh words and treatment, they repeat the pattern with their own children.

It's important to think about the messages you give your child. Are you encouraging self-doubt? Are your expectations too high? Do you respect her feelings? Are you too demanding? Do you say things that make her feel shame and guilt? Are you hard to please? Do you dwell on her weaknesses and take her strengths for granted? Do you spend enough time with her?

Give her more verbal rewards. Praise her capabilities ("You can pour your own milk!") and accomplishments ("You built that tower by yourself."), and point out her talents ("You learned that song!") and endearing traits ("You're so nice to your sister."). Ignore or minimize her faults. Encourage her when she tries new activities, and offer support when she needs it.

When you treat your child in positive ways, she'll feel good about herself. This will help her build confidence. As she grows, improved self-esteem will help your child feel happier, more satisfied, and more successful.

What can I do about lying?

"I'm not doing anything." "I didn't hit him." "I already went to the bathroom."

The "minor" lies children tell often involve things they don't want to do, such as brush their teeth or take a shower. A child will say, "Yes, I washed my hands," when she hasn't, or "I didn't eat any cookies," when she has. Kids sometimes don't tell the truth when they want to avoid something they don't want to do. "I already brushed my hair." They also distort the truth, because they don't want to get into trouble or be reprimanded. "I didn't take his ball; he gave it to me."

One five-year-old hid her grandma's keys because he didn't want her to leave: "I don't know where Grandma's keys are!" Young children believe that if they say, "I didn't do it," others will believe him. That's just how preschool-aged children think.

All children are exposed daily to examples of questionable honesty. Parents say, "I'll be off the phone in a minute," and then they talk half an hour longer. Teachers say, "I'll get to you soon," but they leave the child waiting. Television commercials promise exciting toys, but children discover that the products don't actually work or meet expectations. After watching a commercial, one four-year-old said, "They're lying about what that doll does, and you're not supposed to lie." They also hear adults offering false excuses. "I'm so sorry I can't make the meeting tonight, but I'm not feeling well." And many parents, as a way to get their three-year-old to cooperate, will say (with a wink) to their five-year-old, "Pretend that you're going to bed now."

A child isn't lying when he says, "I have five cookies" when he only has two, or "I have that toy, too," when he really doesn't. Young children have strong imaginations, and they don't have a concept of numbers.

The way you talk to your child about lying is important. Instead of asking, "Did you spill the milk?" or "Did you take her toy?" try addressing it differently, "Let's clean up the milk together." "You need to give her the toy back."

Instead of angrily shouting, "You're lying again!" show some understanding of your child's position. Say, for example, "I think you made up that story because you were afraid I'd get mad at you."

A child might distort the truth because he finds his parents' discipline too threatening. If the consequences of misbehaving are very harsh, a child will lie to avoid them. And if parents impose heavy punishments for lying about the misbehavior, he may be even more afraid to admit the truth.

If you've eased up on your reactions and your child's still lying, look at other aspects of his life. Is he having problems in school? Is he able to make friends? Is he getting enough positive attention at home? Observe him at play and ask his teacher for observations and suggestions.

As long as your child's lying isn't excessive, you don't need to worry. Just watch his behavior, reinforce examples of honesty, and continue talking about telling the truth.

Chapter 11

FAMILY LIFE WITH YOUNG CHILDREN

- Why are my children so different from each other?
- How should I deal with the differences between my children?
- Is sibling rivalry normal?
- How can I discourage sibling rivalry?
- Will my child always be jealous of her siblings?
- Is it okay for parents to argue in front of their child?
- How should I handle my child's relationship with his grandparents?
- Is shyness normal?
- Will my shy child be okay at school?
- How can we have fewer problems on long car trips?
- My child doesn't like to lose—how can I help?
- Should I limit TV watching? Video games? Computer time?
- Is it okay if I just want my child to take it easy over the summer?
- How can I be more patient with my child?

Why are my children so different from each other?

Children in the same family can sometimes be strikingly different. Parents may believe they're raising their children in similar ways, yet the children have very different personalities, abilities, and interests. Why?

Naturally, heredity plays a major role in determining temperament and abilities. One child in a family may be easygoing by nature, another more sensitive. One may have athletic ability, while another is intellectually inclined.

Gender affects personality differences as well. Boys and girls frequently have different interests and activity levels, although each may become strongly involved in activities stereotypically associated with the opposite sex. In addition, kids often imitate what they see, and if parents have very different interests and personalities, one child may imitate her mother, while the other follows her father.

The way parents treat their children has a major impact on the development of personality, interests, and abilities. Parents shape and steer their child in many ways, both consciously and unconsciously. They may encourage musical talent while ignoring mechanical ability; they may inadvertently stifle creativity or individuality while urging their child to "be good." They may offer her nurturing role models or help her become a leader.

Within a family, each child's experience is unique. For instance, a firstborn receives a lot of attention during her years as the only child. However, because her parents are inexperienced, they may be cautious, demanding, and nervous at the same time that they're loving and proud. Parents are sometimes a little more relaxed or lenient with their younger children.

There are other circumstances that lead parents to treat their children differently, often with negative results. One child may have a temperamental characteristic that unhappily reminds her parents of something in themselves or another relative. Parents don't like seeing familiar negative characteristics reflected in their child and may wish—or pressure—her to be different.

The resemblance can be something specific. A parent with a strong temper may single out a child with a similar personality. "Your loud mouth will get you in trouble." The parent who has negative feelings about himself may treat the child who is like him more harshly than he treats his other children.

The resemblance can also be general. A child might simply be a reminder to her parents that they (and she) are not as aggressive, talented, or intelligent as they would like to be. One parent, talking to his spouse about their child, said, "She's stubborn, just like you."

If one child physically resembles a parent or other relative in a way that makes parents uncomfortable, they may voice their displeasure. "Your hair is so thin, just like my sister's." "You have ears like your mother." "You're short like me." More often parents don't mention their feelings aloud, yet still may be bothered by aspects of their child's appearance.

The child who is the unfortunate target of such comments will feel unhappy and singled out among her siblings. If she hears these messages often enough, she'll internalize them. "I'm not smart." "I'm not pretty." "I'm not good at sports." She may behave as though what she's heard is true. Her siblings who have escaped their parents' criticism will not have such negative self-images.

Siblings may also develop strong differences if one seems to be favored by her parents. For example, if parents believe one child is prettier than the other and express that belief to both, one will grow up feeling worthwhile, while the other will feel less valued and less attractive.

Sometimes parents focus too much attention, time, or money on one child; this can have a negative impact on the other children in the family. If a child sees her brother receive attention and praise for his athletic ability, she'll look for a way to get attention for herself. She may try to compete with him, but that's unlikely if she feels she can't match him. Rather than risk having her parents compare her performance to his, she may eventually give up on sports altogether.

Instead, she'll try to find another way to distinguish herself. She may try art or dancing, or develop a charming or funny manner. However, if she can't get enough positive attention from her parents, she might seek negative attention, perhaps developing a behavioral problem at home and school. As time goes on, the unhappier she becomes, the more likely she is to become careless with her schoolwork, family, and peers, and the less likely she'll be to get positive feedback from her parents. Her experience will be very different from her sibling's.

Parents sometimes deliberately steer their kids in different directions, often to avoid possible conflicts and competition. If an older child enrolls in dance class, her parents may discourage her younger sibling from doing the same for fear one will outshine the other. Some parents were raised in competitive households and want to spare their children the experience of failing to measure up to a sibling. However, when parents keep one child from pursuing her interest, they rob her of a chance for enjoyment and accomplishment.

Siblings can successfully participate in the same activities as long as their parents don't focus on competition between them or praise one and not the other. Even if one is better, there will always be something good to say about each. Both should be encouraged.

How should I deal with the differences between my children?

Although it's intriguing and important to consider the differences between your children, it's also important to deal with the differences carefully. Accept each as she is, nurture her, and encourage her to pursue activities that she enjoys and is good at. Don't push and pull her in directions she can't or doesn't want to go. Remember not to compare your children out loud. They'll hear your comparisons as judgments, and one will end up feeling superior or inferior to the other.

It's natural to feel disappointed in your children at times. "He's not the ball player I'd hoped he'd be." "I wish she were more sociable." Try to accept what disappoints you. It's emotionally unhealthy for your children to hear your negative evaluations. They'll wonder, "What's wrong with me?" "Why couldn't I be like my sister?"

The best way to treat differences is matter-of-factly and with respect. "Sam enjoys reading." "Julie likes gymnastics." Your kids will be affected throughout their lives by the way you view them. If you set the right tone, they'll follow your lead and learn to appreciate and accept differences as a natural part of life. As a result, they'll grow up feeling good about their siblings and themselves.

Is sibling rivalry normal?

Parents are far too accepting of sibling rivalry; many excuse it. "That's just how kids are. All brothers and sisters fight." Many stop trying to deal with it because they don't know what to do. They hear the endless bickering, whining, and arguing, and just give up, only interfering when one child starts crying or gets physically hurt. Yet parents aren't helpless. There are steps they can take to eliminate most of the day-to-day struggles between siblings.

The key is getting involved. Parents shouldn't ignore their children's rivalry. When kids sense that a parent won't step in, they often escalate their battles. One boy, who was rarely reprimanded for the way he treated his sister, continually picked on her. Some people believe that paying attention to sibling rivalry only encourages it, because kids argue in order to get attention. However, kids generally put their efforts into seeking positive, rather than negative, attention.

The real root of sibling rivalry is a child's angry belief that he isn't being treated fairly, that his sibling is enjoying more parental affection or privileges. He directs his anger toward his sibling rather than his parents because he needs his parents for love and care. He doesn't want to risk losing their approval. It's much safer to attack a brother or sister.

A child will feel unfairly treated if his parents say, "Your sister is older, so she gets to stay up later." A child can easily feel hurt and insecure if his parents say, "You need to practice more than your brother does," "Let him show you how to throw the ball," or "Your sister knows how to put that together." The child being praised will feel entitled to gloat and may start to say, "I know how to draw, and you don't," or even repeat his parents' words, "You don't know how to do that." The one being put down will start to resent his sibling.

This presents a dilemma for parents who believe older children should have more privileges. One mother thought her five-year-old should stay up later than her three-year-old. This caused great conflicts. The older child teased the younger, and the younger yelled, "I don't like you!" Eventually, the three-year-old fussed so long at bedtime that he was awake as long as his sister anyway.

If an older child is treated as bigger and better than a younger sibling, the younger will fight for the privileges his sibling enjoys. He'll feel helpless, unequal, and powerless to change what he sees as an unfair situation, and he'll take those feelings out on his sibling.

Many parents can remember their own similar feelings of resentment toward a brother or sister, yet they continue to treat children as they once hated being treated. A better alternative to granting privileges by age is to treat kids equally, and make simple and practical allowances for differences in size, maturity, and physical development.

Sibling rivalry may escalate or develop if a new baby is born. A former "only child" will face the shock of sharing his parents for the first time. A pair of siblings will find their positions in the family altered by the baby's arrival. The middle child, in particular, may feel left out. Parents can ease their older children's adjustment by giving them extra attention and acknowledging their feelings. "It's hard getting used to a new baby, isn't it?"

How can I discourage sibling rivalry?

Whenever you face sibling rivalry in your family, you should talk to your children, clearly stating your expectations. Let them know what the limits are, and discuss ways they can control their fighting. "Let Molly know you're mad without hitting her." "If you don't like what your brother's doing, come tell me and we'll work it out together." "You have to include your sister." If you don't set limits on rivalry, your children will believe you accept their negative behavior, and it will likely continue.

If you catch them in the middle of an argument, make them sit down and discuss the situation with each other or with you. If necessary, act as a mediator. "Mason doesn't want you to grab toys from him." Listen to each child's side, even if that means putting up with, "You played with it longer!" or "No, I had it first!" After you've listened, ask them to come up with a solution: "How can you fix this problem?" Offer a solution yourself, or direct them toward another activity.

Sometimes they'll have trouble talking about their fights. They know they're angry, but they don't know how to explain why. Suggest possible reasons for your child's dissatisfaction. "Maybe you think Nicole got a better toy than you did." "You might be mad because Corey got to watch more TV."

Let your children know that if they persist in arguing, there will be consequences. You already know what will work best, whether it's taking away (or threatening to take away) privileges or sending your child to a "be nice" chair. Make sure the consequences for misbehavior are appropriate and not too harsh, or you'll just stir up more resentment. Instead of thinking, "I won't hit him," your child may be so angry at his punishment that he'll think, "I'm never playing with my brother again!"

You may have success by offering your children rewards for getting along, but be prepared to monitor your children closely. While you might see improved behavior, you also might see an increase in tattling or threats. "Ooh, I'm telling on you, and you won't get a treat from Mom." You might also find that the novelty wears off, and the rewards gradually become less effective.

Above all, to eliminate rivalry, treat your children fairly. If you tend to reward one child and blame the other, reevaluate your attitudes. When you're fair and generous with your praise—"Thank you for sharing with your sister," or "I'm glad you let Billy play with you"—they'll feel better about themselves and be less likely to argue.

Of course, you can never stop all the bickering. "Shut up!" "Stupid!" and "I hate you!" are standard sibling exchanges. They're upsetting, but they're the quick, angry expressions of a sibling relationship. If the bickering is brief, infrequent, and quickly resolved, just accept it. But whenever sibling rivalry moves beyond a few words spoken in haste, step in, set limits, and help your children resolve their differences.

Will my child always be jealous of her siblings?

Every child feels some jealousy toward her siblings. A toddler may be jealous of the attention a new baby receives. A four-year-old may resent an older one's abilities, privileges, and experience. A quiet child may resent the attention her more outgoing or accomplished sibling receives. While some jealousy is inevitable, consistent jealousy comes from a child's belief that she's being treated unfairly (from her point of view) by her parents.

Children are very sensitive to their parents' words and actions: "You always let Tyler play with that." "Mommy always yells at me." "My brother always gets to stay up late." Parents, at times, give more positive attention to one child. Perhaps they feel that he needs encouragement or is temporarily vulnerable: "You were so nice today." They may feel proud of one child's accomplishments: "Show Grandma and Grandpa what you learned in ballet." A child may be right about her treatment, or she may be misreading her situation. But as long as she thinks she's being slighted or not given the attention she needs or wants, she'll be jealous.

Parents' attitudes and actions shape the relationships between siblings. Sometimes, without realizing it, parents favor one child. They may believe they're fair, but in subtle and powerful ways, they give great cause for jealousy: "Becky knows how to pour her own juice. You need my help." "Thank goodness Katie's such an easy baby." "Could you please be a good listener like your brother?"

When kids feel jealousy, they often express it: "You always let her sit there!" However, many parents get angry or won't listen: "That's not true!" "You sit on that chair just as many times as your brother." If a child gets yelled at or in trouble for protesting, she'll stop speaking up. Complaining is risky if it means making parents angry. A child who can't express her feelings to her parents will act out, misbehave, or direct her anger or resentment toward her sibling, which will create sibling rivalry.

There are constructive changes you can make if you want to lessen sibling jealousy: Do the best you can at being fair. Be open to changing your ways, especially if jealousy between your children is significant. Don't take sides or compare them to each other. Don't expect the same behavior from each of your children. Give them the time and attention they need. Try to create a balance so that, despite differences in age, interests, personality, and skills, each of your children feels special and important.

Listen to her suggestions: "Watch me too." "Don't always talk about Ian." When your child sees and experiences changes you make in how you respond to her and her siblings, she'll start to feel better about her siblings, and she'll begin to feel less jealous.

Is it okay for parents to argue in front of their child?

All children are exposed to parents' arguments. Some parents quarrel frequently and openly without considering their children's reactions, and other parents argue in private. Yet none can hide the fact that they disagree. Kids are aware of yelling and arguments going on even behind closed bedroom doors.

When parents argue in front of their child, they may frighten him. He may go to sleep scared and go to school worried. He may also take sides and yell at the parent he believes is at fault. "Stop yelling. Don't keep fighting!"

He may blame himself for his parents' arguments and think, "If I put my toys away, Mommy and Daddy won't be mad." Such wishful, magical ideas are very real and powerful.

If you argue in front of your child, consider his feelings. He'll become quite upset if you and your spouse are loud and insult each other. Control your accusations and unkind words and give thought to the impact your arguments have on him.

Remember that your child considers you a model. Every day, you show him how adults and couples behave. If you and your spouse don't treat each other with respect, if you yell, belittle each other, and argue constantly, your child may eventually copy your behavior.

You may even find that he's imitating your behavior now. If

he's been exposed to frequent blaming and discord, he might treat his siblings in ways you find unacceptable. You may find yourself demanding, "Don't treat your brother that way. That's not nice," or "Don't talk to your sister like that."

If you and your spouse argue frequently, consider seeking professional counseling. When you're able to get along more harmoniously, your entire family will benefit.

How should I handle my child's relationship with his grandparents?

Grandparents can be very special to a child. Many grandparents take an active role in the care of their grandchildren. In a good relationship they offer unconditional love and acceptance. They often pay undivided attention and listen with interest to all that their grandchild has to tell. Many grandparents are flexible— they have free time, and their own lives are fairly settled. Since they don't have day-to-day responsibility for their grandchild, they can get involved without worrying about such tough issues as discipline and education.

Good grandparent-grandchild relationships usually revolve around the child's interests, although children sometimes will listen carefully to their grandparents' stories and may enjoy participating in a grandparent's hobby. Still, the focus is on the child.

Sometimes parents find themselves in the middle of the grandparent-grandchild relationship. In the best of situations, parents love to share their child's accomplishments with grandparents and hear them say wonderful things back. It's especially gratifying when grandparents compliment parents for successful child rearing. But the relationship can be complex and uncomfortable, especially for the generation in the middle.

When grandparents criticize the way their grandchild is being raised, parents resent the intrusion. If grandparents are especially loving towards their grandchild, a parent may angrily or jealously wonder why she didn't experience such acceptance when she was young: "Why are they so nice now? They were never like that when I was growing up." At the other extreme, if grandparents aren't loving enough, parents experience the loss of a relationship they wanted for their child.

If your child's grandparents are intent on seeing and enjoying him, the relationship will flourish. If they're emotionally or geographically distant, there are some things you can do to encourage the relationship.

When grandparents live far away, remain in constant contact via phone, videocam or email. Exchange emails describing recent activities, or send pictures (either hard copies or via the Internet) often. Send DVDs of your child playing, singing, showing off his room, or telling a story. You can help your child write to his grandparents by giving him several addressed, stamped envelopes ready to send off with a drawing, photo, or letter.

If you've kept grandparents at a distance because of their attitudes or actions, or because you think they spoil your child, reconsider your position. One parent who thought her mother overindulged the grandchildren began to see that the leniency and generosity didn't harm them or make them greedy. She began to invite her mother over more often and welcomed her involvement.

If you sense that your child is bothered or worried about his grandparents, let him talk about his feelings. If his grandmother is sick or if there's a sudden change in her health or living situation, he may ask lots of questions and seek reassurance: "Will Grandma always be sad?" "Will we still get to see her?"

The relationship between grandparents and grandchildren can enrich both generations. When it works, it's wonderful. When it doesn't develop as you would wish, there still will be benefits. As the parent in between, try to accept whatever disappointment you feel, and nurture the good parts of the relationship.

Is shyness normal?

Shyness is often viewed as a problem. Many people believe it is an undesirable trait, one that reflects a poor self-image. Actually, it's only a problem when people perceive it as one. A reserved child who is not taught that something is wrong with her, will be just as confident, happy, and involved as her more outgoing peers.

One woman who was shy as a child had parents who never made her feel bad about her quiet nature. As a result, she's a reserved adult who moves confidently through life. Another woman remembers being chastised for her shyness. Her parents constantly tried to change her: "Why don't you act like the other kids?" "Why are you so quiet?" She still feels self-conscious and uncomfortable, and imagines her mother saying, "Talk! Just go ahead and talk to them!"

The way a child perceives her shyness depends mostly on her parents. If they accept her personality and don't focus on shyness as a problem, she will also be matter-of-fact about her shyness. She'll see herself as able to do and enjoy the same things other children do. But if her parents try to change her or focus too much on her shyness, she'll become self-conscious. It's a fine line between acceptance and feeling badly about having this trait. The more parents concentrate on shyness as a problem, the worse their child will feel about herself.

Shyness is a personality characteristic and should be accepted as one, not as a flaw. Reserved children are often nice, well-behaved, and generous. When they get older, they usually become good listeners and enjoy and respect privacy. They also can enjoy watching other children participate in activities. Although they're shy in some circumstances, they may handle situations well. One five-year-old who wanted to try a hula hoop that another child was using told her mother, "At first I was shy, and then I just asked her if I could use it."

Shy children are often fine in small groups of two or three children, or in one-on-one conversations with an adult. A shy child who's involved in an interesting project won't appear shy. It's only when she's being focused on that her shyness becomes apparent.

While shyness should not be seen as a problem for a child, it can be frustrating for parents. They may feel uncomfortable or embarrassed when their child doesn't respond as other children do. They may feel judged, and they may see her ignored by adults who engage with other, more talkative children.

Parents can help themselves and their child by avoiding uncomfortable situations and protecting her when necessary. For instance, many shy children don't like to be put on the spot to say hello or otherwise talk on demand. If she appears unlikely to respond to an adult's questions, her parents should matter-of-factly respond for her and then quickly steer the discussion away from her. The alternative, trying to force her to talk, will only make her feel worse and will probably be ineffective.

If parents expect guests at their home, they can prepare their child or make special arrangements for her. She might feel more comfortable if she has a friend of her own over. She might prefer helping before the guests arrive rather than when the visitors are in the house. If parents generally arrange situations so she doesn't feel focused on, everyone will feel better.

Will my shy child be okay at school?

Parents often wonder how to approach the subject of shyness in school. If that's a concern of yours, wait and see how comfortable your child is in class. Don't begin the school year by telling the teacher your child is shy; the teacher may treat her differently or anticipate problems. If your child feels self-conscious about being made to speak in class, schedule a conference at school. Let the teacher know you don't want your child to receive negative messages about shyness. You have to correct any adult who believes she can change your child's personality.

Many teachers prefer quiet students. Your reserved child may be rewarded for her behavior, perhaps more than you would wish. One shy kindergartner received stickers at school for being so "good" and quiet. Then, during a school conference, the teacher told the parents the girl was very shy. "But you reward her for being quiet!" her parents replied. They asked the teacher to stop reinforcing her shy behavior and instead reward her for finishing her work or participating in class.

Sometimes your child will come home from school or play feeling frustrated because she couldn't participate comfortably. She may become whiny or demanding. Accept that she needs understanding and an outlet for her feelings. If she feels comfortable enough, she may talk to you about shyness and how it sometimes interferes with activities. Certainly as she gets older, an accepting atmosphere at home will make it easier for her to share her thoughts.

You may be convinced that your child will always be shy, but it's hard to predict the path she'll take. Some kids who are extremely shy during the preschool and elementary years may gradually become more outgoing. In any case, your job is to accept your child as she is and help her find activities and situations that make her feel good.

How can we have fewer problems on long car trips?

"How much longer?" "I wanna get out of my car seat!" Traveling by car with children can be a challenge. They get bored and restless when confined to a small space for hours, and siblings forced to sit with each other often end up arguing and whining. It takes advance planning and patience for travel to go relatively smoothly.

Try to make the drive as physically comfortable as possible. Have your child bring a blanket, and be sure she's wearing comfortable clothes. Have her wear shoes she can take off during the ride and quickly get into for short stops.

As much as possible, time your travels to coincide with your child's schedule. Early morning and late evening are usually calm times for young children, and she may sleep if you drive those hours. Plan plenty of stops for snacks or exercise. If someone else is driving, sit it in the back with her when she needs your involvement.

Listen together to the radio or a CD, or let her watch a DVD. Sing together or play "I Spy." If you're able to read while riding, pick a story to read aloud to the family.

Pack several small, lunch-size bags for her to have in the car, some with food and some with things to do, and give her one when she seems bored, tired, or upset along the way. The food bags can contain drinks and a variety of snacks that can be easily handled. To avoid extra tension and conflicts, don't demand neatness or get angry when she makes crumbs or spills juice. Carry a battery oper- ated car vacuum or put small towels around her car seat and on the floor so the mess can be easily cleaned up.

The "fun" bags can include toys, stickers, small-sized books, a video game (and extra batteries), and a family photo book. Periodically during the trip you may want to give her small, wrapped, surprise gifts geared to her interests. She'll enjoy opening them, and the novelty will keep her attention. Have her put some toys and activi- ties in her own backpack.

Any new toy, game, or interesting object will hold your child's atten- tion for a while, but if the trip is long, you'll eventually hear, "Are we there yet?" Children ask this question over and over again because they don't have an adult understanding of time or distance. It's best to be prepared to answer this question many times, in a calm way. And whether you say, "We'll be there soon," or "We'll be there in one hour," your answer should not be fueled with frustration or anger, "I already told you!" "Stop asking me that question!" Sitting for long periods of time is difficult for young children and they're excited to get to the destination. With patience and planning, you can avoid major conflicts and keep your child reasonably content for most of your drive.

My child doesn't like to lose—how can I help?

Parents of a preschooler know that games are not always fun. A young child often insists on playing by her own rules and gets upset if she loses. This typical preschool behavior can make it difficult for you and your child to genuinely enjoy playing games. It takes time, often not until the kindergarten years, for children to show better control over their feelings, understand the purpose of rules, and no longer focus entirely on the need to win.

Since young children don't like to lose, they'll say, "I don't want this card," or "I'll tell you when it's your turn." They also spontaneously change rules so they can win: "From now on let's say you can bounce the ball twice." At these ages, children can't put themselves in another person's position and understand that others want to win just as they do.

Game playing is essentially a social activity. However, young children aren't able to consistently cooperate with each other enough to always play fairly. Also, they can't think carefully about others' moves, anticipate other players' actions, and prepare for a possible loss or a quick recovery. They don't have the cognitive know-how to do these things—yet.

If you want playing games with your child to be fun, you'll probably have to play by her rules. If you argue with her ("Hey, you already had your turn," or "If you cheat, I'm putting the game away"), you're taking playing games too seriously.

It's okay to accommodate your child's desire to win. And don't worry—she'll follow other adult guidelines in school or at a friend's home if she's required to. As she matures, it'll be more enjoyable to play games with her, because she'll have an easier time handling the competition in games and following rules. That's just how development works.

In the meantime, don't get angry or mean-spirited when you lose. Be a good example of how to handle disappointment and a positive example of good sportsmanship.

Should I limit TV watching? Video games? Computer time?

Children enjoy watching TV and playing video and computer games. Parents are often ambivalent and worried about these occupations. They want their child to be happy, they welcome the peace that comes when he's occupied, and yet they consider many programs, games, and websites a waste of time or ones that send a wrong message.

How can you balance your feelings and your child's desires? You can begin by considering the appeal of TV, games, and the computer. Children relax in front of the TV, just as many adults do. Appropriate programs are entertaining or at least diverting. Even commercials are interesting to a child. The toys look inviting, and young children are easily convinced by a sales pitch: "That truck really climbs mountains."

Video and computer games interest children for a number of reasons. They're exciting, challenging, and action-filled. A child works on the skills that help him win, such as visual-motor and small-muscle coordination. Games offer immediate feedback in the form of points and new action, and a child always has the option to start over if he loses or doesn't like the way a game's going.

When a child plays these games, he feels powerful. He's controlling characters that fight and capture each other, win sports contests, or go on mysterious quests. It's easy to see how attractive this is to a child who spends most of his day being controlled by others. In school or day care the teacher tells him how long he has to eat lunch, when to go outside, and what to do. At home, parents are in charge. But while playing a video or computer game, a child has power.

The appeal of the computer is obvious to adults. Kids visit interesting and fun sites filled with characters they see in books and on TV. They can dress up dolls with fancy clothes, sing along with Barney, use arts software, do puzzles, and become exposed to new and intriguing things and activities.

But there are problems with TV, games, and computers. Their content is often violent or simply not nice, has sexual undertones, or is otherwise inappropriate for young children. Parents have to put limits on the kinds of shows, video games and websites their child is exposed to. When deciding what's appropriate for your child, trust your judgment, and err on the side of caution, since children take in information differently than adults do. Parental controls can help parents protect their child.

Even without content problems, video and computer games can be very frustrating for children these ages. A child may work on a game for a long time, only to lose and have to start all over. Parents sometimes hear screams of anger from a child who can't take the pressure or frustration. When he has trouble dealing with this aspect of game playing, he may take his feelings out on whoever's closest. "Get out of here!" "Don't talk!" When children are upset about their games, they don't often get sympathy from their parents. "If you're this upset, why do you play?"

Watching TV has its own negative effects. Children may be confused and upset because they're not always sure what's real or made up, and they accept as fact much of what they hear about disasters, sickness, and violence, as well as what they see about relationships and how people treat each other.

After a disturbing program or misleading show, a child needs reassurance and answers to his questions. Unfortunately, parents are often not watching with him and may not be available to help. Even when they are, he may still be exposed to disturbing or uncomfortable sights that remain with him. One child worried continuously after seeing news clips of an earthquake. A five-year-old saw passionate kissing on TV and said, "Is that their real lips touching? Ooh. That's so gross."

There's another problem related to this issue: Children who spend too much time watching TV, playing video games, and being on the computer have less time for creative play and being with their families. Some children spend time watching and playing video games because they can't think of anything else to do. In such cases, parents should offer alternatives such as time with a playmate, reading aloud, drawing, painting, using play dough, building a block structure, playing imaginative games, or going to a playground.

Parents take many different approaches to controlling TV, the computer, and video games. Some forbid their use on weekdays, and some set a precise time limit.

Some parents set no limits, instead using TV, games, and the computer to occupy their child. As long as he's quiet and out of the way, they don't regulate this time at all. While all parents occasionally resort to these activities to keep kids busy, it's harmful to give children total control over how they occupy their time.

You can limit your child's TV watching, computer use, and video-game playing without setting up a strict schedule. Take a flexible approach. Allow longer playing time when he has a new game. Extend TV viewing hours during weekends and holidays or when a special show is on. Cut back when you want him involved in other activities.

Try to avoid having him stop in the middle of a program he's involved in watching. He'll become frustrated, "It's not over yet," and won't understand your line of reasoning, "You're watching too much TV." Instead tell him, "After Dora, I'm turning the TV off, and we're going outside."

Factors such as the weather and sickness will also help determine how much viewing, computer time, and game playing you'll allow. Your goal is to strike a balance between his wish to spend time on games and shows (ones you've okayed), and your desire to see him use his time more productively.

Is it okay if I just want my child to take it easy over the summer?

A child's summer doesn't have to be filled with camp and organized activities. Some parents decide not to send their children to camp at all, opting instead for a relaxed, unstructured few months. This works best for parents who can tolerate a loose schedule and follow their child's lead, and who don't mind a day without plans. Parents who prefer more structure or who can't let their child stay home because of work schedules can still set aside some free summer time for the family to take it easy together.

With guidance and supervision, children can find enjoyable things to do at home or in the neighborhood. Kids can play in sprinklers, plant a garden, fly kites, play with sand, play hopscotch, draw a chalk design on the sidewalk, skate, build a fort, go to playgrounds, or ride a bicycle. Kids can play with friends, play alone, take swimming lessons, or do things with the family. They can continue recreational classes and lessons they took during the school year.

Summer is an important time for families. Schedules are often less hectic, and there are more opportunities to be together. Even if both parents work, longer daylight hours leave evenings more open. If parents have errands, they can take their child along and include time for an ice cream stop. If they have to work over the weekend, they can take him with them and let him work at something too.

While your child is home, his friends may be off at camp; this won't be a problem if he can occupy himself. But if he gets bored or lonely, you should help him find activities to get involved in. You may also decide to compromise and send him to camp for part of the summer, letting him have the rest of the summer free.

How can I be more patient with my child?

Parents' impatience takes several forms. One is situational—they lose their tempers and snap at their child for his misbehavior. A second form is more general. They lack the patience to listen to him, play with him, get involved in his interests, set limits calmly, or help him learn to read. Impatience can have a negative impact on children and make parents feel guilty.

All parents lose patience at times, especially when they're rushed or busy or feeling badgered by their children's demands. "I've got to get to work." "I'm trying to pay bills. Don't make so much noise." "I can't read to you right now." Parents experiencing stress at home or at work are especially likely to snap at their child.

Such impatience due to circumstances is often mild and temporary. More harmful is constant criticism and rudeness. Parents with a low tolerance for frustration may routinely yell at their children, ridicule them, and call them names. "Don't be so messy! I've told you a hundred times to put your toys away." "I'm tired of you whining." "Hurry up! You're so slow."

Parents with high expectations and a strong desire to be in control can become intolerant when things don't go their way. They expect too much cooperation. If their child can't meet their standards, they react with harsh impatience. In the process, they may hurt his self-confidence, harm family relationships, and cause him to become less, rather than more, cooperative as he copies the treatment he's received.

In less dramatic ways, parents also show impatience when they neglect to make time for their child. It takes a reordering of priorities to put aside adult concerns and answer a child's question, look at his art project, take him on a walk, sit on the floor and play with him, read a book to him, and genuinely take an interest in his activities. Even the busiest parents can stop what they're doing several times a day to concentrate on their child. But some parents—even ones with time to spare—don't make their child's needs and interests a priority.

Becoming a more patient parent takes purposeful effort and may require a change in attitude, priorities, or behavior. If you're easily frustrated, try to make your life less stressful by easing up on your expectations. It's more important to spend time with your child than to have a clean house. It's better to stay calm during the early evening than to prepare a complex dish for dinner. If work or family problems are difficult to cope with, you may find stress-reduction techniques useful. You can learn about them from books, magazines, or classes.

Think about your tone of voice when you talk to your child—try using the same tone you'd like him to use. Don't shout, put him down, roll your eyes in frustration, or put your hands on your hips and say, "I'm waiting!" The more you take your child's feelings into consideration, the better his behavior is likely to be. In the long run, he'll respond more positively to your calm words than to rude orders.

Make a decision to spend more time with your child. Put your book or work down, stay off the phone and computer at night, turn the TV off, forgo some evening plans, and get involved with him. This is not always easy, since it means giving of yourself without necessarily receiving an immediate return. But there are definite benefits. Your child will have you as a model of more tolerant, patient behavior. He'll feel better about himself because you're interested in him. And the relationship between the two of you and your family will improve.

Index

About the Authors

Robin Goldstein, PhD, is a nationally known parent educator, specialist in child development, and faculty member at John Hopkins University. Her advice has appeared in *Redbook, Working Mother, Good Housekeeping*, and other national publications. She is a frequent guest on TV and radio and is a popular corporate speaker. As a parenting consultant, Robin advises families on their everyday challenges and helps parents understand their young children's behavior.

Janet Gallant is the author of books and articles on a wide range of subjects including health, education, business, and public safety. She has also written numerous publications for federal government agencies. Janet is the author of the popular book *Simple Courtesies*. She lives in Rockville, Maryland.

3x   12/15

2X   1 eln House
        5/2011